D0898181

Heinemann Plays

The Cherry Orchard

Heinemann Plays

The Cherry Orchard

Anton Chekhov

English Version by
Sir John Gielgud

with an Introduction by
Michel Saint-Denis

Heinemann
London

Theatre Arts Books
New York

Heinemann Educational Books Ltd
22 Bedford Square, London WC1B 3HH

LONDON   EDINBURGH   MELBOURNE   AUCKLAND
HONG KONG   SINGAPORE   KUALA LUMPUR   NEW DELHI
IBADAN   NAIROBI   JOHANNESBURG
EXETER (NH)   KINGSTON   PORT OF SPAIN

ISBN 0 435 20160 3

First published 1963
Reprinted 1965, 1968, 1969, 1972, 1976, 1979, 1981
First published in the *Heinemann Plays* Series 1984

Printed and bound in Great Britain by
Spottiswoode Ballantyne Ltd,
Colchester and London

THE CHERRY ORCHARD

This version was made for a production which I directed at the Lyric Theatre, Hammersmith, in 1954. Madame Marie Britnieva gave me help and advice on many details and subtleties of meaning. In 1961, the version was used again by Michel Saint-Denis for the Royal Shakespeare Theatre Company production at the Aldwych Theatre. For this production Madame Suria Magito went over the text with me and suggested a number of valuable revisions. I am most grateful to these two Russian ladies for their help and enthusiasm.

J.G.

Introduction

by

Michel Saint-Denis

WHY DO we produce successive translations of the same work, and particularly of Chekhov's plays?

Is it not, first of all, because the authentic value of a written text which deserves to become classical can only be found in the original? A translation may reach the very heart of a foreign language, it may give in its own terms a perfect equivalent to a foreign style; it amounts to a re-creation, it has the authority of the original. This kind of achievement is extremely rare.

Most of the time, a translation keeps the colour of the period in which it has been written, a foreign colour, and it feels old-fashioned to the younger generations. The original may be dated in its own way; the translation, however, has no authority, it is open to discussion – and theatre people are always keen to discuss their texts, particularly in the case of a text supposed to be 'realistic', colloquial.

Here we touch on the difficulty of translating Chekhov. My Russian friends tell me that Chekhov's use of words, of expressions, of syntax, amounts to poetry, without any formality; so that, to them, the occasional intrusion of a modern English colloquialism is bound to break the spell. Chekhov's prose is deceptive: of easy approach, it is extremely sensitive; it is not everyday language, but seems to be; difficult to decipher, it is the language of 'souls', of feelings, of moods; anything too immediate may disturb it.

The present version by Sir John Gielgud represents a new attempt at rendering the original text, carefully studied, in ordinary but sensitive English.

The interpretation of a play like *The Cherry Orchard* presents difficulties of a similar kind. It is impressionistic art and you can't take any written line at its face value. The elementary meaning is given by the very story told by the play: the theme is simple, but it is played upon, from act to act, in so many ways, by so many characters, in so many shades, that its material aspect disappears; the story is a pretext, well chosen, to make us discover with great discretion, through the poor lives of a group of people, ruthlessly but charitably observed, an unforgettable vision of laughable, suffering and lovable humanity.

Story and characters, however, are placed in a definite social context; the selling of the cherry orchard is made unavoidable by the carelessness and impotence of its owners, but, because Russian society is beginning to change, this simple fact takes a meaning of new significance. 'The most beautiful place on earth' is passing from the hands of rural gentry to those of a self-made man whose grandfather was a serf on the estate: the new owner will demolish the house, cut the cherry orchard down, divide the land into plots for 'vulgar' summer villas and visitors. The event is no more, in 1904, than a sign, the announcement of a revolution which is not to take place for many years; so that the reactions of the characters to it are varied, uncertain, unstable, even for Lopahin, who is both proud and ashamed of what he has done and cannot believe it is true. Among the others, the young welcome 'the new world', some are indifferent, or affected only in their emotions and their livelihood; the victims are the old masters, their adopted daughter and their manservant: they are not aware of any social significance in what has happened to them and, a month before being 'forgotten', dying, Firs calls the emancipation from serfdom 'the great calamity'. Any clear-cut classification of the characters would be misleading; everyone reacts from his own situation and feelings: Yasha wants to return to Paris because 'this is a barbarous country', even the 'revolutionaries' in the bud, Trofimov and Lopahin, behave as unstable human beings much more than as doctrinaires. In spite of the worries and dissatisfactions which isolate from each other the characters and their definite individualities, they communicate, they still belong to the same world. It is a world which is disintegrating, however, and most of them, more or less consciously, with their loves, their selfishness, their ideals, their ridicules, their charm, are beginning to suffer the tortures of the great change which is going to tear them from their past.

It seems to me that such were the spirit, the meaning and the style of the play when Chekhov wrote it. The world of Madame Ranevsky was still the present; the old society was still alive, with its luxury, its privileges, its reassuring traditions; its beauty also, and around it the misery, the ignorance, the complacent backwardness of the people. Chekhov, as a doctor and as a writer, is the informed witness of this stage of things. There is no doubt where he stands; however objective in his appreciation of human beings and facts, he belongs to the group of liberal intellectuals from whose midst the revolution is going to be slowly and passionately prepared but in 1904, for the Russian nation, the idea of a change is vague; it is a matter for hope, distant expectation, mixed in different degrees with apprehension and fear.

Today, not only is the Russian revolution nearly half-a-century old, but, outside Russia, everybody who is not blinded by hate or prejudice recognizes that it has been a necessary evil and the life of the Russian people is now beginning to be transformed for the better. The words of Vershinin in *The Three Sisters*, those of Trofimov and Lopahin in *The Cherry Orchard*, announcing happiness in the future, may still be exaggerated or even ironical, but they have now a much more positive value than twenty or thirty years ago. To me it is a matter of fact and not of interpretation; the characters who represent the 'new world' have grown in stature; they are neither prophets nor heroes, as the Russians represent them in their new productions, but they have, naturally, a much greater impact on a contemporary audience than before. At the same time, the Ranevsky-Gaev world has receded into a remote past, where silliness and artificiality cannot be redeemed by generosity or innocence, by frankness in the confession of human weakness, or by the romantic attachment we like to feel for the golden old days.

Finally, I find justification in the insistence with which Chekhov went on repeating that *The Cherry Orchard* was not a tragedy, but 'a comedy, even a farce'. If this is so, at whose expense should we mostly laugh? Epihodov's, Dunyasha's, Charlotta's, Pishtchik's evidently, Firs's here and there, but the list is too short; we may add to it some moments of

Trofimov, 'the eternal student', and most of Gaev. If, however, we underline the beauty of the disappearing past, through the sets and costumes, together with the charm, warmth and elegance of Madame Ranevsky, if we mark the brutality of Lopahin more than his youth and clumsiness, how shall we succeed in sounding the note of comedy?

To me, Madame Ranevsky represents the past in its most vulnerable aspect: in her hands is the balance of the comedy. Laughter can only come from the contrast between the terrible state of affairs in which Madame Ranevsky finds herself as a mother and a woman of good upbringing, and her irresponsible and light-hearted behaviour in her love and business affairs; charm in that case should not so much help emotion as increase the enjoyment of comedy.

It is obvious, however, that these views do not allow a producer to ignore the quick changes of mood which are natural to Russian people and essential to the completeness of Chekhov's characters. Between emotion and comedy a point of balance has to be found, but *The Cherry Orchard* has, more than any other play by Chekhov, its well established traditions in England. The 'connoisseurs' have fallen in love with the scenery, with the dear creatures, representing the threatened past; they mock Trofimov and have little sympathy for Lopahin; they were bound to resent the degradation of romantic values purposely displayed in my recent production. The contradictions of the Press contributed to the liveliness of the public's reactions; some complained they were not moved enough while others regretted not being given more opportunities to laugh. It is my belief and my hope that our interpretation has brought many people, particularly among the young, to a new understanding of this many-sided masterpiece.

CHARACTERS
(in order of appearance)

LOPAHIN, Yermolay Alexeyevich	a merchant
DUNYASHA	the maid
EPIHODOV, Semion Panteleyevich	a clerk on Madame Ranevsky's estate
FIRS	an old servant, aged 87
MADAME RANEVSKY, Lyubov Andreyevna	a landowner
ANYA	her daughter, 17 years old
CHARLOTTA IVANOVNA	a governess
VARYA	Mme Ranevsky's adopted daughter, 24 years old
GAEV, Leonid Andreyevich	Mme Ranevsky's brother, aged 51
PISHTCHIK, Semyonov	a landowner
YASHA	a young manservant
TROFIMOV, Pyotr (Petya) Sergeyevich	a student
A PASSER-BY	
A STATIONMASTER	
A POST-OFFICE CLERK	
A GOVERNMENT OFFICIAL	
GUESTS, SERVANTS, etc.	

The action of the play takes place on the Estate of Madame Ranevsky.

ACT ONE: A room in the house. May. Dawn.

ACT TWO: In the fields. July. Sunset.

ACT THREE: The drawing room. August. Evening.

ACT FOUR: As Act One, the same room. October. Morning.

This version of THE CHERRY ORCHARD *was first performed at the Lyric Theatre, Hammersmith, on 21 May 1954. It was presented by Tennent Productions Ltd with the following cast:*

LOPAHIN	Trevor Howard
DUNYASHA	Charlotte Mitchell
EPIHODOV	Robert Eddison
FIRS	Hugh Pryse
MADAME RANEVSKY	Gwen Ffrangcon-Davies
ANYA	Shirley Roberts
CHARLOTTA IVANOVNA	Patience Collier
VARYA	Pauline Jameson
GAEV	Esme Percy
PISHTCHIK	George Howe
YASHA	John Bennett
TROFIMOV	David Markham
A PASSER-BY	David Dodimead
STATION-MASTER	David Dodimead
POST-OFFICE CLERK	Gareth Morgan

The Play directed by
JOHN GIELGUD

Sets and Costumes designed by
RICHARD LAKE

This version of THE CHERRY ORCHARD *was presented by the*
Royal Shakespeare Theatre Company at The Aldwych Theatre,
London. It opened on 14 *December* 1961 *with the following cast:*

LOPAHIN	George Murcell
DUNYASHA	Patsy Byrne
EPIHODOV	Patrick Wymark
FIRS	Roy Dotrice
MADAME RANEVSKY	Peggy Ashcroft
ANYA	Judi Dench
VARYA	Dorothy Tutin
GAEV	John Gielgud
PISHTCHIK	Paul Hardwick
CHARLOTTA IVANOVNA	Patience Collier
YASHA	David Buck
TROFIMOV	Ian Holm
A PASSER-BY	Gordon Gostelow
COACHMEN	Russell Hunter
	Peter Holmes
GARDENER	Julian Battersby
STABLE BOY	Michael Warchus
STATION-MASTER	William Wallis
HIS WIFE	Narissa Knights
GOVERNMENT OFFICIAL	Michael Murray
SCHOOLMASTER	Ronald Scott-Dodd
HIS WIFE	Rosemary Mussell
POST-OFFICE CLERK	Gareth Morgan

The Play directed by
MICHEL SAINT-DENIS

Sets designed by
ABD'ELKADER FARRAH

ACT ONE

SCENE: *A room, which to this very day is called the nursery. One of the doors leads to Anya's room.*

Dawn. Soon the sun will rise. It is the beginning of May; the cherry trees are in bloom, but it is cold in the garden; early morning frost. The windows of the room are closed.

DUNYASHA *comes in with a candle.* LOPAHIN *is half-asleep in a chair; he has a book in his hand.*

LOPAHIN: The train's in, thank Heaven. What time is it?

DUNYASHA: Nearly four o'clock. (*Blows out the candle.*) It's getting light already.

LOPAHIN: I wonder how late the train is? Two hours, at least. (*Yawns and stretches.*) What a fool I am! Nice mess I've made of things, I must say. I came here on purpose to go to meet them at the station, and suddenly dozed off and fell asleep – sitting up in the chair. How annoying . . . you ought to have woken me up.

DUNYASHA: I thought you'd already gone. (*Listens.*) There, I do believe I can hear them coming.

LOPAHIN (*listens*): No. What with getting the luggage out and one thing and another. . . (*Pause.*) Lyubov Andreyevna has lived abroad for five years; I wonder what she's like now ... she used to be a fine woman, so easy and simple in her ways. I remember, when I was a lad of fifteen, my old father – he worked in a shop in the village in those days – punched me in the face with his fist and made my nose bleed. We were here in the yard together, I forget what we'd come about. Lyubov Andreyevna – she was still very young in those days, and so slim – took me up to the wash-stand in this very room, here in the nursery. 'Don't cry, little peasant,' said she, 'it will heal by your wedding day.' ...(*A pause.*) Little peasant – it's true my father was a peasant and here I am in a white waistcoat and brown shoes, like a bull in a china shop. . . . Well, I'm rich now with stacks of money. All the same if you stop to think about it, once a peasant always a peasant. (*Turns over the pages of the book.*) I was reading this book, not understanding a word of it. Fell fast asleep. (*A pause.*)

DUNYASHA: The dogs have been barking all night, they know their mistress is coming home.

LOPAHIN: What's the matter, Dunyasha, you're so . . .

DUNYASHA: My hands are trembling. I feel quite faint.

LOPAHIN: You try to be too refined, that's your trouble, my girl, dressing up, with your hair all done like a young lady's. You ought to remember your place.

    EPIHODOV *comes in with a bunch of flowers; he wears a pea-jacket (short coat) and highly polished top-boots, which squeak loudly at every step. He drops the bunch of flowers as he comes in.*

EPIHODOV (*picking up the bunch of flowers*): Here, the gardener sent these, says they are to go in the dining-room. (*Gives* DUNYASHA *the bunch of flowers.*)

LOPAHIN: And bring me some kvass.

DUNYASHA: Very well. (*Goes out.*)

EPIHODOV: Three degrees of frost this morning and the cherries all in bloom. I can't say much for our climate. (*Sighs.*) I really can't. Our climate is not altogether very propitious, so to speak. Yermolay Alexeyevich, permit me to remark that the day before yesterday I bought myself a new pair of boots, and I take the liberty to assure you they squeak quite abominably. What ought I to grease them with?

LOPAHIN: Leave me alone. I'm sick of you.

EPIHODOV: Every day some misfortune happens to me, but I can't complain. No, I've got used to it, I can even smile.

　　DUNYASHA *comes in, and hands* LOPAHIN *the kvass.*

Well, I'll leave you now. (*Stumbles against a chair which falls over.*) There! (*As though triumphant.*) There, you see. What a cataclysm, if you'll pardon the expression! As a matter of fact – it's positively remarkable. (*Goes out.*)

DUNYASHA: You know, Yermolay Alexeyevich, I must tell you, Epihodov has made me a proposal.

LOPAHIN: Ah!

DUNYASHA: I really don't know what to do about it. . . . He's a decent fellow, but once he starts talking you can't understand a thing he says. It all sounds very nice and touching, but you can't understand anything. I think I rather like him. He loves me desperately. He's an unlucky fellow; every day something seems to happen to him. They tease him so in the kitchens – they call him twenty-two misfortunes. . . .

LOPAHIN (*listening*): There! They're coming I think. . . .

DUNYASHA: Yes. So they are – oh! Whatever's the matter with me – I'm cold all over!

LOPAHIN: They're really coming. No mistake about it. Let's go and meet them. Will she recognise me, I wonder? We haven't seen each other for five years.

DUNYASHA (*in a flutter*): I'm going to faint. . . . Oh! I shall faint, I know I shall.

One hears two carriages drive up to the house. LOPAHIN *and* DUNYASHA *go out quickly.*

The stage is empty. A noise begins to be heard in the neighbouring rooms. FIRS, *who has driven to meet* MADAME RANEVSKY *at the station, crosses the stage hurriedly, leaning on a stick. He is dressed in an ancient livery and top hat. He mutters something to himself, but one cannot understand a single word. The noise off-stage is growing. A voice* (ANYA'S): Come, let's go in here.

Enter LYUBOV ANDREYEVNA, ANYA *and* CHARLOTTA IVANOVNA *with a little dog on a chain; all three are dressed in travelling clothes.* VARYA, *in a coat with a handkerchief on her head,* GAEV, SEMYONOV-PISHTCHIK, LOPAHIN, DUNYASHA, *with a bundle and an umbrella, servants with luggage. Everyone passes across the room.*

ANYA: Let's go through here. You remember this room, Maminka?

LYUBOV ANDREYEVNA (*joyfully, through her tears*): The nursery!

VARYA: How cold it is, my hands are quite frozen. (*To* LYUBOV ANDREYEVNA.) Your rooms are just as they were, Mamma, the white room and the mauve one.

LYUBOV ANDREYEVNA: The nursery, my dear beautiful room. . . . I used to sleep here when I was little. (*Cries.*) I'm behaving like a little girl still. (*Kisses her brother and* VARYA, *and then her brother again.*) And Varya still looks like a nun, just the same, just as she always did. And I recognised Dunyasha at once. (*Kisses* DUNYASHA.)

GAEV: The train was two hours late. What do you think of that? Terrible state of affairs.

CHARLOTTA IVANOVNA (*to Pishtchik*): My dog even eats nuts.

PISHTCHIK (*in wonderment*): Good gracious! Think of that! *They all go out except* ANYA *and* DUNYASHA.

DUNYASHA: We've been waiting and waiting for you. . . . (*She takes off* ANYA'S *hat and coat.*)

ANYA: I haven't slept for four nights on the journey. . . . I'm frozen to death.

DUNYASHA: It was Easter when you went away. There was snow then and frost. But now . . . my precious! (*Laughs happily and kisses* ANYA.) How I've missed you, waited for you, dearest, my pretty one! Oh, I must tell you something at once. . . . I can't keep it to myself a moment longer. . . .

ANYA (*feebly*): What is it now?

DUNYASHA: Just after Easter, Epihodov, the clerk, made me a proposal!

ANYA: It's always the same with you. . . . (*Arranging her hair.*) Oh! All my hairpins have fallen out. . . . (*She is so tired that she almost staggers.*)

DUNYASHA: I really don't know what to do about it. He loves me, he loves me so much!

ANYA (*looks tenderly towards her door*): My own room, my window, just as if I'd never been away. I'm home! To-morrow morning I shall wake up and run into the garden.... Oh! If only I could get to sleep! I never slept all through the journey, I was so anxious.

DUNYASHA: Pyotr Sergeyevich arrived the day before yesterday.

ANYA (*joyfully*): Petya!

DUNYASHA: Yes, he is sleeping out in the bath-house, lives there, too. 'I'm afraid of being in the way', he said. (*Glancing at her pocket watch.*) I ought to go and wake him up, but Varvara Mikhailovna told me not to. 'Don't you wake him', she told me.

VARYA *enters with a bunch of keys hanging from her belt.*

VARYA: Dunyasha, get some coffee, quickly. Mamma wants some.

DUNYASHA: Yes, at once. (*Goes out.*)

VARYA: Well, thank God you've arrived. You're home again. (*Caressing her.*) You're really here! My darling. You've come back to me, my precious.

ANYA: You've no idea what I've been through.

VARYA: I can just imagine.

ANYA: I left here in Holy Week – it was cold then – and Charlotta would keep chattering all the time and showing-off her conjuring tricks. Why on earth did you want to go and tie Charlotta round my neck?

VARYA: You couldn't travel alone, ANITCHKA – not at seventeen!

ANYA: Well, we arrived in Paris. It was so cold, and there was snow on the ground. I can't speak a word of French. Mamma was living on the fifth floor of a big house. I went upstairs, and there were a lot of French people with her—ladies, and an old Catholic priest with a book. The room was full of tobacco smoke, and very uncomfortable. I suddenly felt sorry for Mamma, oh, so sorry, I took her face in my hands and couldn't bear to let her go. Mamma kept on kissing me, and crying. . . .

VARYA (*through her tears*): Don't . . . don't. . . .

ANYA: You know she had to sell her villa at Mentone, she has nothing left, nothing. And of course I hadn't a kopek either, we could hardly manage to get home. And Mamma won't understand! Whenever we got out to have dinner at a station she would order the most expensive things and tip the waiter a whole rouble. Charlotta's just the same. And Yasha expects an expensive dinner too. It's simply awful. You remember Yasha, the boy Mamma took with her for a manservant, she's brought him back with her.

VARYA: I've seen the young rascal.

ANYA: Well, how is everything here? Has the interest on the mortgage been paid off?

VARYA: There's nothing to pay it with.

ANYA: Oh dear, oh dear!

VARYA: The estate is to be sold in August.

ANYA: Oh, heavens!

LOPAHIN: (*peeps in at the door and moos like a cow*): M-mmoo. . . (*He goes.*)

VARYA (*through her tears*): I'd like to. . . (*Shakes her fist.*)

ANYA (*embracing* VARYA, *gently*): Varya, has he proposed to you, yet?

> VARYA *shakes her head.*

Why? but I'm sure he loves you. Why don't you come to an understanding? What are you waiting for?

VARYA: I don't think it will ever come to anything. He has a lot to do, he has no time for me . . . he doesn't even look at me. . . . May God bless him – but I'd rather not see him; it makes me miserable. . . . Everyone keeps talking about our wedding, everyone keeps congratulating me, and really, there's nothing to it . . . it's just a dream. (*Changes her tone.*) You've got a new brooch like a bee.

ANYA (*sadly*): Yes, Mamma bought it for me. (*Goes to her own room and says gaily and rather like a child.*) When I was in Paris I went up in a balloon!

VARYA: My darling is home again.

> DUNYASHA *has already returned with the coffee-pot, and is making coffee.*

(*Standing at the door to Anya's room.*) You know – all day long, as I'm going about my housework, I dream and dream. If only we could marry you to some rich man then my mind would be at peace, and I would go away somewhere, to a holy place – to Kiev – to Moscow – and I would go on and on – from one holy place to another. Oh, what a wonderful life. What happiness.

ANYA: The birds are singing in the garden. What time is it?

VARYA: It must be after four. It's time you were asleep. (*Entering Anya's room.*) What happiness.

> YASHA *comes in with a rug and a travelling bag.*

YASHA (*crosses the stage, affectedly*): May one pass through this way, mademoiselle?

DUNYASHA: I hardly recognised you, Yasha. How you've changed abroad!

YASHA: H'm ... and who are you, may I ask?

DUNYASHA: When you left here five years ago I was only about so high. (*Shows distance from floor.*) Dunyasha, Feodor's daughter. . . . Don't you remember?

YASHA: H'm. . . . You little cucumber! (*He looks round, and embraces her; she shrieks and drops a saucer.*)

YASHA *goes out hurriedly.*

VARYA (*in the doorway, in a cross tone*): What's going on in here?

DUNYASHA (*through her tears*): The saucer – I broke it.

VARYA: Well they say that's lucky.

ANYA (*coming out of her room*): We ought to warn Mamma that Petya's here.

VARYA: I've told them not to wake him.

ANYA (*deep in thought*): You know it's six years since Father died, and only a month later poor brother Grisha was drowned in the river. Only seven years old and so sweet. It was too much for Mamma, she had to go away, right away, without looking back. (*Shuddering.*) If only she knew how well I understand her. (*Pause.*) Petya Trofimov was Grisha's tutor, he might remind her. . . .

FIRS *comes in; he is wearing a jacket and a white waistcoat.*

FIRS (*very preoccupied, he goes over to the coffee-pot*): The mistress is going to take coffee here. (*Putting on white gloves.*) Is coffee ready? (*Sternly to* DUNYASHA.) You, girl! Where's the cream?

DUNYASHA: Oh! Goodness gracious. . . . (*Hurries out.*)

FIRS (*fussing round the coffee-pot*): Eh . . . you muddler. (*Mutters to himself.*) They've arrived from Paris. . . . The master once went to Paris . . . by coach. . . . (*Laughs.*) Horses all the way.

VARYA: What's that, Firs?

FIRS: Beg pardon? (*Happily.*) My mistress has come back. I've lived to see the day! Now I'm ready to die. (*Weeps with joy.*)

> *Enter* LYUBOV ANDREYEVNA, GAEV *and* SEMYONOV-PISHTCHIK, *the latter in a peasant's coat made of fine broadcloth, with full trousers and top-boots.* GAEV, *as he comes in, makes the gestures of playing billiards both with his arms and body.*

LYUBOV ANDREYEVNA: How does it go? Let me think. . . . Pocket the white! Double into the centre.

GAEV: Pocket the red! Years ago, you know, sister, when we were children, we used to sleep in this very room, side by side, and now I'm over fifty – strange as it may seem. . . .

LOPAHIN: Yes, time flies.

GAEV: What's that you say?

LOPAHIN: Time flies, I say.

GAEV: Somebody's been using cheap scent in here! Patchouli!

ANYA: I'm going to bed now. Good-night, Mamma. (*Kisses her mother.*)

LYUBOV ANDREYEVNA: My precious! (*Kisses her hands.*) Are you glad to be home? I can hardly believe it.

ANYA: Good night, uncle.

GAEV (*kissing her face and hands*): God bless you, little Anya!

How like your mother you are! (*To his sister*.) At her age you were exactly like her, Lyuba.

ANYA *shakes hands with* LOPAHIN *and* PISHTCHIK, *then goes out, shutting the door after her.*

LYUBOV ANDREYEVNA: She's tired out.

PISHTCHIK: It certainly must have been a long journey.

VARYA (*to* LOPAHIN *and* PISHTCHIK): Well, gentlemen! It's nearly five o'clock, time to go home.

LYUBOV ANDREYEVNA (*laughs*): You're just the same as ever, Varya. (*Draws her to her and kisses her.*) I'll drink some coffee, then we'll all be off.

FIRS *puts a cushion under her feet.*

Thank you, dear old friend. I love my coffee, I drink it day and night. Thank you, you dear old Firs.

VARYA: I must see whether they've brought everything in. . . . (*Goes out.*)

LYUBOV ANDREYEVNA: Is it true? Am I really sitting here? (*Laughs.*) I feel I could jump and wave my arms about. (*Putting her hands to her face.*) What if I am only dreaming? . . . God knows I love my country, I love it dearly. I couldn't see out of the carriage window, I was crying so. (*Through her tears.*) All the same, I must drink my coffee. Thank you, Firs, thank you, you dear old man. I'm so glad to find you're still alive.

FIRS: The day before yesterday.

GAEV: He's rather deaf.

LOPAHIN: I have to leave for Harkov almost directly . . . . Such a nuisance – I just wanted to get a glimpse of you first, have a chat. . . . You're just as handsome as you always were.

PISHTCHIK (*breathing heavily*): Better looking than ever and dressed like a Parisian . . . completely bowled me over.

LOPAHIN: Your brother, Leonid Andreyevich, says I'm a money-grubbing peasant. Well, let him say what he likes. I don't care a damn what he says. All I want is that you should trust me as you used to and look at me as you used to in the old days with those big melting eyes of yours. Merciful God! My father was your father's serf and your great-grandfather's before him, but you were so good to me when I was young that I've forgotten all that. I love you like a sister – as if you were my own flesh and blood.

LYUBOV ANDREYEVNA: I can't sit still, I can't do it. (*Jumps up and walks about in violent agitation.*) I suppose it's ridiculous to be so happy. . . . Laugh at me, I'm absurd, I know . . . my darling old bookcase. (*Kisses bookcase.*) My dear little table.

GAEV: Old Nurse died while you were away.

LYUBOV ANDREYEVNA (*sits down and drinks coffee*): Yes, I know, God be with her. God rest her soul.

GAEV: Anastasy is dead, too. Cross-eyed Petrushka has left us now and works in town at the police inspector's. (*Takes a box of caramels out of his pocket and sucks one.*)

PISHTCHIK: My daughter Dashenka . . . sends her greetings. . .

LOPAHIN: I'd like to tell you something agreeable, something cheerful. (*Glancing at his watch.*) I must leave at once . . . there's no time to talk . . . well, I'll say it in two or three words. You already know that your cherry orchard is to be sold to pay your debts. The 22nd of August is fixed for the auction, but don't you worry, my dear lady, sleep in peace, there's a way out. . . . This is my proposition. Now, please listen carefully, I beg you. Your estate is only fourteen miles from town, the railway passes close by, and, if the cherry orchard and the fields along the river were divided into plots and let for building summer villas, you would have an income of at least twenty-five thousand roubles a year.

GAEV: Come, come, my friend, you're talking utter nonsense.

LYUBOV ANDREYEVNA: I don't understand what you mean, Yermolay Alexeyevich.

LOPAHIN: You can ask twenty-five roubles a year at least for every single acre that's let, and, if you advertise in the newspapers at once, I promise you by the autumn there won't be a single plot vacant – they'll all be snapped up. In a word, you're saved. Congratulations. The site is perfect, the river is deep, good for bathing too. Of course, there'll be a lot of clearance to be done – all the old buildings, this house for instance, which is really no use to anyone, will have to go, we must cut down the cherry orchard –

LYUBOV ANDREYEVNA: What did you say? My dear man, excuse me, but you don't understand. If there is one thing really interesting, really remarkable, in the whole neigh-bourhood, it is our cherry orchard.

LOPAHIN: The only remarkable thing about the orchard is that it is a very big one. The trees only bear fruit once every two years, and then nothing can be done with the fruit, nobody wants to buy it.

GAEV: Our orchard is actually mentioned in Andreyevsky's Encyclopaedia.

LOPAHIN (*glancing at his watch*): If you don't think of some-thing practical, then on the 22nd of August both the cherry orchard and your whole estate will be put up for auction.

Make up your minds! I assure you there is no other way out. None whatever.

FIRS: In the old days, forty or fifty years ago, they used to dry the cherries, bottle them, preserve them and make jam with them; and sometimes the cherries . . . were . . .

GAEV: Shut up, Firs.

FIRS: Sometimes the cherries used to be dried, and sent in cart-loads to Moscow and Harkov. They sold well, too. They managed to keep them soft and juicy and fragrant. . . . They knew some way in those days. . . .

LYUBOV ANDREYEVNA: Why don't they do it now?

FIRS: They've forgotten. Nobody remembers.

PISHTCHIK (*to* LYUBOV ANDREYEVNA): What about Paris? What was it like there? Did you eat frogs?

LYUBOV ANDREYEVNA: Crocodiles.

PISHTCHIK: Fancy that . . . you don't say so.

LOPAHIN: Up to just recently there were only the gentry and their peasants in the country, but now in the summer visitors are beginning to arrive. All the towns, even the small ones, are today surrounded by summer villas and more and more people are wanting them. At present these people are content to just sit on their verandahs and drink tea, but gradually, in twenty years' time, say, they will take to cultivating, to working, each his own plot of ground, and then your cherry orchard will have made way for something really valuable and productive.

GAEV (*indignant*): Poppycock!

    Enter VARYA *and* YASHA.

VARYA: There are two telegrams for you, Mamma. (*Chooses*

the key and opens the old cupboard with a loud creak.) Here they are.

LYUBOV ANDREYEVNA: They are from Paris. (*Tears up the telegrams without reading them.*)

GAEV: Do you know how old this bookcase is, Lyuba? Last week I took out the bottom drawer, and when I looked carefully, I found a date burnt inside it. This bookcase was made exactly a hundred years ago. Well, just imagine that. One could celebrate its centenary. Obviously an inanimate object, of course, but all the same, whatever you say, it's a historic bookcase.

PISHTCHIK (*surprised*): A hundred years! Fancy that.

GAEV: Yes. . . . It is remarkable. . . . (*Feels bookcase*), Dear, deeply respected silent friend! I salute your existence, which has for more than a hundred years inspired such shining ideals of goodness and justice; your silent call to profitable study has never failed during all these hundred years, to uphold, (*in tears*) through the succeeding generations of our family, courage, faith in a better future, and a sense of the noble ideals of good behaviour and social consciousness. (*Pause.*)

LOPAHIN: Yes. . . .

LYUBOV ANDREYEVNA: You haven't changed, Leonid.

GAEV (*a little embarrassed*): Off the ball on the right, into the pocket! Red to the centre!

LOPAHIN (*looking at his watch*): Well, it's time for me to go.

YASHA (*handing* LYUBOV ANDREYEVNA *some medicine*): Perhaps you will take your pills now.

PISHTCHIK: You shouldn't take medicine, dear lady. It does

you neither harm nor good. Give them to me, honoured lady. (*Takes the pill box, pours them into the palm of his hand, blows on them, puts them into his mouth and swallows them with a glass of kvass.*)

LYUBOV ANDREYEVNA (*frightened*): But you must be mad!

PISHTCHIK: There! I've swallowed all the pills!

LOPAHIN: What a glutton!

Everyone laughs.

FIRS: The gentleman stayed with us at Easter, and ate half a pail of salted cucumbers. . . . (*Mutters.*)

LYUBOV ANDREYEVNA: What is he muttering about?

VARYA: He's been mumbling like that for the last three years. We've got used to it.

YASHA: Anno domini!

CHARLOTTA IVANOVNA, *very thin, in a white dress, well-corseted, with a lorgnette at her belt, crosses the stage.*

LOPAHIN: Charlotta Ivanovna, excuse me, I haven't time to pay my respects. Permit me. (*Wants to kiss her hand.*)

CHARLOTTA IVANOVNA (*taking away her hand*): If one allows people to kiss one's hand, they begin wanting to kiss one's elbow next, and then one's shoulder. . . .

LOPAHIN: I'm out of luck today!

Everyone laughs.

Charlotta Ivanovna, show us a conjuring trick!

LYUBOV ANDREYEVNA: Yes, do, Charlotta, show us one of your tricks!

CHARLOTTA IVANOVNA: No, thank you, I'm sleepy. I'm off to bed. (*Goes.*)

LOPAHIN: We will meet again in three weeks' time. (*Kisses* LYUBOV ANDREYEVNA'S *hand.*) Until then, good-bye, it's time for me to go. (*To* GAEV.) Good-bye. (*Kisses* PISHT-CHIK.) Good-bye. (*Shakes hands with* VARYA, *then with* FIRS *and* YASHA.) I don't want to go. (*To* LYUBOV ANDRE-YEVNA.) If you think it over and decide anything about the villas, let me know; I can then get a loan of fifty thousand roubles for you. Do think seriously about it, won't you?

VARYA (*angrily*): Oh do go, for heaven's sake.

LOPAHIN: I'm going, I'm going. (*Goes off.*)

GAEV: Counter-jumper! Oh, I beg your pardon. . . . Varya is going to marry him, he's Varya's young man.

VARYA: There's no need to say things, like that, uncle.

LYUBOV ANDREYEVNA: Well, Varya, I'd be very pleased. He's a good man really.

PISHTCHIK: Yes, one must admit he's a good fellow. And my Dashenka . . . says that . . . she says . . . all sorts of things. (*Snores, but wakes up immediately.*) But all the same, most respected lady, lend me . . . lend me two hundred and forty roubles . . . tomorrow to pay the interest on my mortgage.

VARYA (*alarmed*): There's no money to give you, none whatever.

LYUBOV ANDREYEVNA: It's quite true, I really haven't got any.

PISHTCHIK: It'll turn up somehow. (*Laughing.*) I never lose hope. One minute I think that all is lost, that I'm ruined – then suddenly the railway is built across my land and . . . they pay me for it. Something else is sure to turn up, if not today, then tomorrow. . . . My Dashenka will win two hundred thousand . . . she's got a ticket in the lottery.

LYUBOV ANDREYEVNA: I've finished my coffee. Now we can go to bed.

FIRS (*brushing* GAEV *and talking to him like a child*): You've put the wrong trousers on again! Whatever am I to do with you?

VARYA (*softly*): Anya's asleep. (*Opening the window quietly.*) The sun's risen, it's not cold now. Look, Mamma! How lovely the trees look! And the air's so fresh! Listen, the starlings are singing.

GAEV (*opening another window*): The orchard is all white. You haven't forgotten, Lyuba? Our long avenue – how it used to shine – stretching away like a white ribbon on moonlight nights! You remember? You've not forgotten?

LYUBOV ANDREYEVNA: Oh! My childhood! My happy, innocent childhood! I used to sleep in this nursery, every morning when I woke I loved looking out into the orchard, and it was just the same then as it is now. Nothing has changed! White blossoms everywhere! Oh, my orchard! After the dark sad days of autumn and the cold of winter you are born again, fresh and beautiful and gay – God has touched you once more – He's not forgotten you – oh! If only I could free myself from this heavy burden that weighs me down – if only I could forget the past!

GAEV: Yes! And this orchard will be sold to pay our debts, however impossible it may seem.

LYUBOV ANDREYEVNA: Look, there's our darling Mother walking in the orchard . . . in a white dress. Look! It *is* Mamma, surely. There she is! Look!

GAEV: Where?

VARYA: Don't . . . don't!! O God forgive us!

LYUBOV ANDREYEVNA: There's no one really. It only looked like it. To the right there where the path turns off to the summer house, there's a little white tree that bends over and looks just like a woman. . . .

Enter TROFIMOV *in a shabby student's uniform. He wears spectacles.*

How exquisite the orchard is! That mass of white blossom against the blue sky. . . .

TROFIMOV: Lyubov Andreyevna!

She turns towards him.

I only wanted to welcome you, and then I'll go at once. (*Kissing her hand passionately.*) They told me not to come till morning but I couldn't bear to wait.

LYUBOV ANDREYEVNA *looks at him without recognising him.*

VARYA (*through her tears*): It's Petya Trofimov.

TROFIMOV: Grisha's old tutor . . . have I really changed so much?

LYUBOV ANDREYEVNA *embraces him and cries quietly.*

GAEV (*embarrassed*): Now, now, Lyuba.

VARYA (*crying*): You see, I told you, Petya. If you'd only waited till tomorrow.

LYUBOV ANDREYEVNA: My Grisha, my little boy . . . Grisha . . . my son. . . .

VARYA: What can one do, Mamma? It was God's will.

TROFIMOV (*quietly, through his tears*): Don't . . . don't. . . .

LYUBOV ANDREYEVNA (*crying quietly*): My son died . . . he was drowned. Why? What was the use? (*Softer.*) Anya's asleep there, and I'm talking too loudly . . . making such a noise. . . . But tell me, Petya? Why have you grown so ugly? Why do you look so old?

TROFIMOV: An old woman in a railway carriage called me a scruffy-looking fellow.

LYUBOV ANDREYEVNA: You used to be quite a boy, a charming young student, but now your hair is getting thin – and you wear spectacles. Are you still a student? (*Going towards the door.*)

TROFIMOV: It looks as if I shall be a perpetual student.

LYUBOV ANDREYEVNA (*kissing her brother and then VARYA*): Well, go to bed. . . . You have aged too, you know, Leonid.

PISHTCHIK (*following her*): Yes, yes, time for bed. . . . Urgh! My gout. I'll stay the night here . . . Lyubov Andreyevna, my dear soul, early tomorrow morning I must have two hundred and forty roubles.

GAEV: Always the same old story.

PISHTCHIK: Two hundred and forty roubles . . . to pay the interest on my mortgage.

LYUBOV ANDREYEVNA: I haven't any money, my dear friend.

PISHTCHIK: I will return it, dear lady . . . such a trifling sum.

LYUBOV ANDREYEVNA: Well, all right; Leonid will give it to you. . . . You give him the money, Leonid.

GAEV: Give it to him! Certainly not.

LYUBOV ANDREYEVNA: It can't be helped. Give it to him. He needs it. He'll give it back.

LYUBOV ANDREYEVNA, TROFIMOV, PISHTCHIK *and* FIRS *go out and* GAEV, VARYA *and* YASHA *remain.*

GAEV: My sister hasn't lost her old habit of squandering money. (*To* YASHA.) Keep your distance, young man, you smell of the chicken house.

YASHA (*with a grin*): You are always the same, Leonid Andreyevich, just as you used to be!

GAEV: What's that? (*To* VARYA.) What did he say?

VARYA (*to* YASHA): Your mother has come up from the village. Since yesterday she's been sitting in the servant's quarters. She wants to see you. . . .

YASHA: Ech! Why can't she leave me alone?

VARYA: You shameless fellow.

YASHA: What's the hurry? She could just as well have come tomorrow. (*Goes out.*)

VARYA: It's true. Mamma is just the same. If she was allowed to do as she liked, she would give everything away.

GAEV: Yes. (*Pause.*) If doctors prescribe too many remedies for an illness it probably means that the illness can't be cured at all. I think . . . I wrack my brains, I find all sorts of solutions to our problems, so many, in fact, that it means in reality there are none. It would be nice to inherit a legacy from someone, or to marry our Anya to a very rich man, or to go to Yaroslav and try my luck with the Countess, my aunt. She is very, very rich, you know, my aunt.

VARYA (*crying*): If only God would help us.

GAEV: Oh, don't start snivelling, Varya. My aunt is very rich, but she doesn't like us for several reasons. First of all my sister married a solicitor instead of a nobleman. . . .

ANYA *appears in the doorway.*

Then, not only did she marry beneath her but her behaviour since then hasn't been exactly *comme il faut*. Of course, she is a good, kind, charming creature and I love her very much, but, even making every excuse for her, one can't deny that she's a bit immoral – you can see it in her slightest movement.

VARYA: Hush! Anya is standing in the doorway.

GAEV: What's that? Who? (*Pause.*) Funny, something has got into my right eye . . . I can't see properly. And on Thursday when I was at the District Court. . . .

ANYA *comes right in.*

VARYA: Why aren't you asleep, Anya?

ANYA: I can't sleep, I just can't.

GAEV: My darling. (*Kissing* ANYA'S *face and hands.*) My little girl. . . . (*Through his tears.*) You are not my niece, you are my guardian angel, you are everything to me. Believe me, trust me.

ANYA: I do believe you, uncle. Everybody loves you, and respects you . . . but dear uncle, you ought to be silent, you ought to hold your tongue. What were you saying just now about my mother, about your own sister? Why did you say that?

GAEV: Yes. Yes, I know. (*Covering his face with his hands.*) Really, it is awful! Heavens! Oh heavens, help me! And just now I began to make that ridiculous speech about the book-case . . . so stupid of me. And it was only when I had finished speaking that I understood how stupid it was.

VARYA: It's true, uncle, you ought to be silent. Don't talk, that's all.

ANYA: If only you didn't talk so much it would be so much happier for you.

GAEV: Yes, yes, I won't talk any more – I won't. (*Kisses* ANYA'S *and* VARYA'S *hands.*) Only one thing I must say, it's business. On Thursday I was at the District Court, and a lot of people came up to me and began to talk about this and that and the other, and it seems it is possible to arrange a loan without security, so as to be able to pay the arrears on the mortgage.

VARYA: If only God would help us!

GAEV: On Tuesday I'll go in again and talk about it again. . . . (*To* VARYA.) Varya, you must stop caterwauling. (*To* ANYA.) Your mother will speak to Lopahin; of course he won't refuse her. . . . And as soon as you are rested you shall go to Yaroslav to the Countess, your great-aunt. We'll operate from three points at once and *voilà!* We'll pay the interest. I'm convinced. . . . (*Puts a sweet in his mouth.*) On my honour! I swear on anything you like, the estate shall not be sold! (*Excitedly.*) I swear by my happiness. Here's my hand, call me a dishonest, useless person if I allow it to go to auction! I swear it shan't be sold. It shan't!

ANYA (*having become calm and happy*): Uncle, you are so good and clever. (*Embraces him.*) I feel so much better now, calmer and happier.

    FIRS *comes in.*

FIRS (*reproachfully*): Leonid Andreyevich, have you no fear of God? When are you goin' to bed?

GAEV: At once, at once, go along, Firs! I'll get myself undressed. Well, children, bye-bye. . . . Details tomorrow, but now let's go to bed. (*Embraces* ANYA *and* VARYA.) I am a man of the eighties . . . people criticise those old days, but I must say I have had to suffer a great deal for my convictions in my time. That's the reason the peasants love me. One must know the peasants! One must know from what. . . .

ANYA: Now, uncle! What did you promise? There you go again. . . .

VARYA: You know you promised, uncle.

FIRS (*angrily*): Leonid Andreyevich.

GAEV: Coming. Coming. Off to bed. Double into the centre! A good break.

> GAEV *goes out*, FIRS *hobbling after him*.

ANYA: I feel happier now. I don't want to go to Yaroslav and I don't like my great-aunt, but all the same I'm happier, thanks to Uncle Leonid. (*Sitting.*)

VARYA: We must get some sleep. I'll go. Oh! While you were away there was trouble in the servants' quarters. As you know, only the old servants live there; Efimyushka, Polya and Yevstigney—and Karp too. Well, they began to allow tramps and disreputable people in to sleep for the night, if you please. I said nothing. Then I heard that a rumour had gone round that I ordered them to be fed on nothing but peas. Out of meanness, you understand. . . . It was all Yevstigney's doing, of course. All right, I said to myself. Just wait. At last I sent for Yevstigney. (*Yawns.*) In he comes. Now then, Yevstigney, I said, you old wretch, how dare you say such things about me. (*Glancing* at ANYA.) Anitchka! (*A pause.*) She's asleep. (*Taking* ANYA *by the arm.*) Let's go to bed. Come along. (*Leading her.*) My darling's asleep! Come along, now. Come along.

They go.

In the distance beyond the orchard a shepherd is playing on his pipe. TROFIMOV *crosses the stage and, seeing* VARYA *and* ANYA, *stops.*

VARYA: Tccc . . .! She's asleep, asleep. . . . Come, my own.

ANYA (*softly, half-asleep*): I'm so tired. Listen to the bells . . . Uncle . . . kind . . . Mamma and uncle. . . .

VARYA: Come, my darling, come.

Going into Anya's room.

TROFIMOV (*tenderly*): My sunshine! My spring!

CURTAIN

ACT TWO

SCENE: *Fields. An old, tumbledown and long abandoned chapel; beside it a well, large stones, that were once, it seems, tombstones, and an old seat. one sees the road leading to Gaev's property. On one side rises a dark group of poplars; there is the beginning of the cherry orchard. In this distance is a row of telegraph poles, and far, far away on the horizon one sees indistinctly the outlines of a big town, which can be seen only in very fine, clear weather.*
  It is nearly sunset.

CHARLOTTA IVANOVNA, YASHA *and* DUNYASHA *are sitting on a seat.* EPIHODOV *is standing beside them and playing the guitar. Everyone is sitting plunged in thought.* CHARLOTTA *is in an old forage cap; she has taken a gun from her shoulder and is arranging the buckle on the strap.*

CHARLOTTA IVANOVNA (*thoughtfully*): I have no real passport of my own, I don't know how old I am, but it always seems to me that I am still very young. When I was little my father and mother used to travel about from one fair to another, giving performances, and very good ones too. I used to do the 'salto mortale', and all sorts of tricks. When father and mother died, a German lady took me to live with her and began to educate me. Good. I grew up and then became a governess. But where I came from and who I am – I don't know. . . . Who my parents were – I don't know. Perhaps they weren't even married. (*Takes a cucumber out of her pocket and begins to eat it.*) I don't know anything. (*A pause.*) I want to talk so much, but there's no one to listen. . . I've no one.

EPIHODOV (*playing the guitar and singing*):
> What is this noisy world to me;
> What matter friends and enemy. . .

How pleasant it is to play on the mandoline!

DUNYASHA: That's a guitar, not a mandoline. (*Looks in the mirror and powders herself.*)

EPIHODOV: To a man who's mad with love, this is a mandoline. (*Continues to sing.*)
> If once the flame of my love was shared,
> My heart would burn. . . .

YASHA *joins in, humming.*

CHARLOTTA IVANOVNA: How vilely these people sing. . . . Fiu! Like jackals howling.

DUNYASHA (*to* YASHA): All the same, you are lucky to have been abroad.

YASHA: Certainly. I'm bound to agree with you. (*Yawning and afterwards lighting a cigar.*)

EPIHODOV: It stands to reason. Abroad, things attained the height of apotheosis years ago – I mean to say, it's all been going on for ever so long.

YASHA: Obviously.

EPIHODOV: I'm a man of cultivation. I read all sorts of remarkable books, but nevertheless I cannot, positively, comprehend the true direction of what I really want in life; to put it plainly, do I prefer to live – or shoot myself? However, just in case, I always carry a revolver in my pocket. Here it is. . . . (*Shows his revolver.*)

CHARLOTTA IVANOVNA: That's done. I'm off now. (*Picking up her gun and slinging it on her shoulder.*) You are a very clever person, Epihodov, you alarm me; women must fall madly in love with you. Brr! All these clever people are so stupid; I have no one to talk to. . . . I'm alone, always alone, I've got no one . . . and who I am, why I exist, I've really no idea. . . . (*Goes slowly.*)

EPIHODOV: To speak frankly and all other considerations apart, I feel I must explain about myself. As a matter of fact, fate treats me quite pitilessly, as a storm behaves to a small boat. I may be mistaken, of course, but if I am, then why did I wake up this morning, for example, and suddenly see a simply colossal spider – as big as that . . . (*showing with both hands*) sitting on my chest. And when I take kvass in order to get drunk, there, at the bottom of the glass I am sure I see something most highly improper, a large cockroach for example. (*Pause.*) Have you ever read Buckle's 'History of Civilisation'? (*Pause.*) I would like to have your attention, Mademoiselle Dunyasha, just for a minute or two.

DUNYASHA: Well, go on. What is it?

EPIHODOV: I would prefer to be alone with you. . . . (*Sighs.*)

DUNYASHA (*embarrassed*): All right – only first bring me my little cape. . . . You'll find it hanging near the wardrobe. . . . It's a bit damp out here.

EPIHODOV: Very well, Mademoiselle . . . I'll go and fetch it, Mademoiselle. . . . Now I know what to do with my revolver. . . . (*Takes the guitar and goes out strumming.*)

YASHA: Twenty-two misfortunes! Between you and me, that man's a perfect idiot. (*Yawning.*)

DUNYASHA: I do hope to goodness he won't shoot himself. (*A pause.*) I have become so nervous lately. I worry all the time. Ever since I was a little girl, I've lived here with the gentry. I have got out of the way of plain living, and my hands are white, like a young lady's. I have become so refined, so delicate and genteel. Everything frightens me. And if you should go and deceive me, Yasha, I don't know what'll happen to my nerves.

YASHA (*kissing her*): My little cucumber. Of course you ought to learn to behave yourself properly. Nothing I dislike more than a girl who can't behave herself respectably.

DUNYASHA: I've fallen terribly in love with you, Yasha you are so well educated, you can talk about everything.

A pause.

YASHA (*yawning*): Ye-es. The way I look at it: if a girl falls in love with someone, I call her immoral. (*Pause.*) How pleasant to smoke a cigar in the open air. (*Listening.*) Some-one's coming . . . it's the mistress and the rest of them.

DUNYASHA *embraces him quickly.*

Quickly, go back to the house as if you'd been down to the river to bathe; don't go that way, they might see you and then they'll think I've been walking out with you. I really can't stand that sort of thing.

DUNYASHA (*coughing softly*): Your cigar has given me a headache. . . . (*Goes away.*)

YASHA *stays, sits near the chapel.*

LYUBOV ANDREYEVNA, GAEV *and* LOPAHIN *come in.*

LOPAHIN: You must make up your minds once and for all – there's no time to be lost. It's perfectly simple. Are you prepared to give up the property and let them build villas or aren't you? Answer in one word: yes or no? Just one word.

LYUBOV ANDREYEVNA: Who's been smoking horrible cigars here . . .? (*Sitting down.*)

GAEV: Really, it has become much more convenient now that they have built the railway here. (*Sitting down.*) We took the train into town for lunch today and here we are back already. White to cannon-off the red. Perhaps I ought to go up to the house first and have a game. . . .

LYUBOV ANDREYEVNA: There's plenty of time.

LOPAHIN: Just one word! (*Pleading.*) Do give me an answer.

GAEV (*yawns*): What do you say?

LYUBOV ANDREYEVNA (*looking into her purse*): Yesterday I still had quite a lot of money, but today I've hardly any left. Poor Varya is trying to economise by feeding everyone on milk soup; the old people in the kitchen get nothing but peas, and yet I can't stop spending right and left. . . . (*Dropping her purse, some gold pieces are scattered.*) Ah, now I've dropped it all, how stupid of me. . . . (*She is vexed.*)

YASHA: Allow me, Madame, I'll pick them up in no time. (*He gathers the money.*)

LYUBOV ANDREYEVNA: Please do, Yasha. And whatever made me go into town for lunch today? That horrid restaurant with its wretched little orchestra, and the table-cloth smelling of cheap soap. . . . Why must you drink so much, Leonid? And eat so much? And talk so much? You never stopped talking in the restaurant today, and what did it all amount to? A lot of nonsense about the seventies, and the decadents. And who was there to listen to you? Fancy talking about decadents to the waiters!

LOPAHIN: Yes, fancy.

GAEV (*waving his hands*): I'm incorrigible, I know I am. (*Impatiently to* YASHA.) What are you doing, dodging about in front of me all the time? Get out of the way, Yasha!

YASHA (*laughing*): I can never hear your voice without laughing.

GAEV (*to his sister*): Either he must go or I shall really . . .

LYUBOV ANDREYEVNA: Go along now, Yasha, be off with you.

YASHA (*gives* LYUBOV ANDREYEVNA *her purse*): I'm going this very minute. . . . (*Hardly able to suppress his laughter.*) *He goes off.*

LOPAHIN: Do you know Deriganov, the millionaire, wants to buy your property? They say he's coming to the auction to bid himself.

LYUBOV ANDREYEVNA: Where did you hear that?

LOPAHIN: They were saying so in the town.

GAEV: Our aunt from Yaroslav has promised to send us money, but we don't know when it will arrive or how much it will be.

LOPAHIN: Well, how much do you think? A hundred thousand? Two hundred thousand?

LYUBOV ANDREYEVNA: Well . . . fifteen or twenty thousand at most, we'd be thankful for that.

LOPAHIN: Excuse me saying so, but in all my life I have never seen such frivolous, scatter-brained, unbusinesslike people as you two. I tell you quite plainly that your estate is going to be sold, and you simply behave as though you didn't understand.

LYUBOV ANDREYEVNA: Well, what can we do? Tell us what to do.

LOPAHIN: I keep on telling you over and over again. Every day I tell you the same thing. You must lease the cherry orchard and the land to build villas. You must do it at once, immediately! Do you understand? The auction will be on us at any moment! Decide once and for all to have the villas, and you will be able to borrow as much money as you want, and then you will be saved.

LYUBOV ANDREYEVNA: Villas and summer visitors! Really! Forgive me, but it's all so vulgar.

GAEV: I agree with you, absolutely.

LOPAHIN: I shall lose control of myself in a minute, burst into tears, or scream or faint. I can't stand it any longer! You're driving me crazy! (*To* GAEV.) You are an old woman! That's what you are.

GAEV: What do you say?

LOPAHIN: I say you're an old woman! (*Wants to go*)

LYUBOV ANDREYEVNA (*frightened*): Now, now, don't go, stay with us, there's a dear. I beg you. Perhaps we will think of something.

LOPAHIN: What's there to think about?

LYUBOV ANDREYEVNA: Please don't go. I want you to stay. Somehow it's gayer when you're here. . . . (*Pause.*)

I am always expecting something to happen, as if the house would tumble down about our ears.

GAEV (*in deep thought*): Double to the centre off the red . . . cross into the middle pocket.

LYUBOV ANDREYEVNA: You know, we have been wicked, sinful people. . . .

LOPAHIN: Sinful? You?

GAEV (*putting a sweet in his mouth*): They say I've eaten up my entire fortune in caramels. . . .

LYUBOV ANDREYEVNA: Oh, I've been such a fool. . . . Look at the way I've always thrown my money about, thoughtlessly, like a mad woman. I married a husband who did nothing but get into debt. He drank himself to death on champagne – he drank terribly – and then it was my misfortune to fall in love with another man; I went away with him, and almost immediately – it was my first punishment, a blow straight to my heart – here, in the river . . . my little boy was drowned. And I went abroad – right away, never to return, never to see this river again. I simply shut my eyes and ran away, blindly. I was almost out of my mind. He followed me and made my life a misery. I bought a villa near Mentone, because he fell ill there, and for three years I knew no rest, night or day. His illness exhausted me, it wore me out. Then, last year, when we sold the villa to pay our debts, I went to Paris and there he robbed me of everything I possessed, left me, and went away with another woman. I tried to poison myself . . . stupid, humiliating. And then I suddenly began to long to be back in Russia, in my own country, with my little girl. . . . (*Wiping her tears.*) O God, be merciful. Don't punish me any more. (*Taking a telegram from her pocket.*) This came today from Paris . . . imploring my forgiveness, begging me to return. . . . (*She tears up the telegram.*) Isn't that music, somewhere? (*She listens.*)

GAEV: That is our famous Jewish orchestra. You remember, four violins, a flute and a double bass.

LYUBOV ANDREYEVNA: Do they still exist? We ought to get them to come up to the house some time. We'll have a dance.

LOPAHIN (*listening*): I can't hear anything. . . . I saw an extremely funny play at the theatre in town last night. (*Humming softly.*) 'And if you pay a Prussian he will Frenchify a Russian'. (*He laughs.*) Most amusing.

LYUBOV ANDREYEVNA: I'm sure it wasn't a bit amusing. You people oughtn't to go to see plays, you should look at yourselves instead and see what dull lives you lead, and what a lot of nonsense you talk.

LOPAHIN: It's perfectly true. I must admit our lives are stupid. . . . (*Pause.*) My father was a peasant, an idiot, he understood nothing, taught me nothing, and beat me with a stick when he was drunk. Actually I'm just the same, just another blockhead, another idiot. I've learnt nothing either. My handwriting is awful, I'm even ashamed to let people see how bad it is. I write like a pig, and I'm ashamed of it.

LYUBOV ANDREYEVNA: You ought to get married, my friend.

LOPAHIN: Yes . . . that's true.

LYUBOV ANDREYEVNA: You ought to marry our Varya, she's a good girl.

LOPAHIN: Yes.

LYUBOV ANDREYEVNA: Though she's not my own daughter, she comes of good honest stock, you know, and she's such a hard working creature, she loves to be working all day long. And above all she loves you. You know you've always seemed to like her.

LOPAHIN: Well, I'm quite agreeable . . . she's a good girl. (*Pause.*)

GAEV: They're offering me a job in the bank, at six thousand roubles a year. Have you heard?

LYUBOV ANDREYEVNA: What's the use . . . ? Stay as you are.

FIRS *comes in with an overcoat.*

FIRS (*to* GAEV): Please be so good as to put this on, master, it's getting damp.

GAEV (*putting on his coat*): What an old nuisance you are, Firs.

FIRS: It's all very well, but this morning you went off and never told me – (*Examines him.*)

LYUBOV ANDREYEVNA: How old you've got, Firs!

FIRS: What did you say?

LOPAHIN: We were saying you've aged a great deal.

FIRS: I've been alive a long time. They were going to marry me off before your father was born. . . . (*Laughs.*) I was first footman before the freedom was granted, but I didn't take my freedom and stayed with my masters. . . . (*Silence.*) I remember when everyone was glad. What they were glad about nobody really knew.

LOPAHIN: Oh, yes. Those were fine days all right. There was good flogging then anyway.

FIRS (*not hearing*): I should think so. A peasant was a peasant, and a master a master, but now everything's topsy-turvy; there's no understanding any of it.

GAEV: Be quiet, Firs. Tomorrow I must go to town, I've been promised an introduction to some general or other who might lend us some money.

LOPAHIN: Nothing will come of that. And you wouldn't be able to pay the interest anyway.

LYUBOV ANDREYEVNA: He's talking nonsense, there is no general, he's just making it up.

Enter TROFIMOV, ANYA, *and* VARYA.

GAEV: Look, here come the children.

ANYA: Here she is! Here's Mamma!

LYUBOV ANDREYEVNA (*embraces* ANYA *and* VARYA): Come here, my darlings, if only you knew how much I love you both. Sit beside me here, now we're comfortable.

Everybody sits down.

LOPAHIN: Our perpetual student is always out with the young ladies.

TROFIMOV: It's none of your business.

LOPAHIN: He'll be fifty soon, and he's still a student.

TROFIMOV: Stop making idiotic jokes.

LOPAHIN: What are you losing your temper for?

TROFIMOV: Why can't you leave me alone?

LOPAHIN: Let me ask you one question, what do you really think of me?

TROFIMOV: My opinion of you, Yermolay Alexeyevich, is simply this. You are a wealthy man and you'll soon be a millionaire. Just as a wild beast who devours everything that crosses its path is necessary to the pattern of life, so you are necessary too.

Everyone laughs.

VARYA: Talk about something else, Petya, tell us about the planets.

LYUBOV ANDREYEVNA: No, let's go on with the conversation we were having yesterday.

TROFIMOV: What was it about?

GAEV: We were talking about pride.

TROFIMOV: We talked for a long time yesterday, but we didn't arrive at any conclusion. You believe there is something mystical in a man of pride. Perhaps you are right, but, if one looks at the thing simply, without any preconceived ideas, what sense is there in pride? Considering that man is not very well constructed physiologically, and, in the vast majority of cases, is stupid, coarse, and profoundly unhappy? We ought to stop all this self-admiration. The only thing to do is to work.

GAEV: We shall die all the same.

TROFIMOV: Who knows! And what does it mean – to die? It may be that man has a hundred senses, and with death only the five we know are lost, while the other ninety-five remain alive.

LYUBOV ANDREYEVNA: How clever you are, Petya!

LOPAHIN (*ironically*): Oh! Extraordinary!

TROFIMOV: The human race progresses, continually perfecting its own powers. Everything that is out of reach to us now will one day be near and clear. Only we must work and help with all our strength those who seek the truth.

Here in Russia only a very few people work at all – and those who call themselves intellectuals seek for nothing, do nothing and seem to be incapable of work. They call themselves intellectuals, but they speak rudely to their servants and treat the peasants as if they were animals. They are not even well read, and they are idle too – talking grandly about science and understanding very little of the arts. They pretend to be serious, theorise about philosophy – but all the same the great majority of them live anyhow, sleep anywhere, in filthy crowded rooms, in dirt and squalor. It is quite obvious that all our well-meaning intentions serve only to mislead both ourselves and others. Where are the nurseries and the libraries we are always promised? People write about them in the novels; in reality they don't exist. Nothing exists but dirt, vulgarity, and the laziness and indifference that are the curse of the Russian temperament. I dislike people with solemn faces. I am afraid of solemn conversations. . . . We'd do better to hold our tongues.

LOPAHIN: Do you know I get up before five every day and work from morning till night? I deal with other people's money as well as my own, and I know what people are like. One only needs to begin to work at something to understand how few honest, decent people there are in the world. Sometimes, when I can't sleep I think, 'Lord God, you have given us these immense forests, great plains and vast horizons, and living here amongst them, we really ought to be giants. . . .'

LYUBOV ANDREYEVNA: Oh dear, you want giants now . . . they are all very well in fairy stories, but in real life they would be rather alarming.

EPIHODOV *passes backstage, playing his guitar.*
(*Thoughtfully.*) There goes Epihodov. . . .

ANYA (*thoughtfully*): There goes Epihodov. . . .

GAEV: The sun has set, dear people.

TROFIMOV: Yes.

GAEV (*quietly, but as a sort of declamation*): O nature, wonderful
nature, glowing with your eternal brilliance, beautiful and
indifferent, light that we call our mother, uniting both life
and death within yourself, you create life and you destroy it.

VARYA (*pleading*): Uncle dear.

ANYA: You are doing it again.

TROFIMOV: You'd much better double the white into the
centre.

GAEV: I'll hold my tongue, I won't say a word.

They all sit in thought. Quiet reigns. You can only just hear
FIRS *mumbling softly. Suddenly there is a far-away noise, as if*
from the sky, the sound of a breaking string.

LYUBOV ANDREYEVNA: What was that noise?

LOPAHIN: I don't know. Somewhere, far away in the mines,
a cable may have broken loose. It must be very far away.

GAEV: Perhaps it was some sort of bird . . . a heron or something.

TROFIMOV: Or an owl. . . .

LYUBOV ANDREYEVNA (*shivering*): It sounded uncanny
somehow. (*Pause.*)

FIRS: The same thing happened before the great calamity;
the owl screeched and the samovar kept hissing.

GAEV: What calamity?

FIRS: When they gave us freedom. (*Pause.*)

LYUBOV ANDREYEVNA: Come along, my friends, it's getting dark, let's go in. (*To* ANYA.) There are tears in your eyes. . . . What is it, my little girl? (*Embracing her.*)

ANYA: Nothing, Mamma, it's nothing.

TROFIMOV: Someone's coming.

A PASSER-BY *appears in a white cap and a coat, he is slightly drunk.*

PASSER-BY: Excuse me, can I get through to the station this way?

GAEV: You can. Follow the road.

PASSER-BY: Much obliged to you, sir. . . . (*Coughing.*) Glorious weather we're having. . . . (*Declaiming.*) Brother, my suffering brother . . . pull on the oars . . . the swollen Volga moans. . . . (*To* VARYA) Mademoiselle, please spare something for a poor suffering fellow-countryman. . . .

VARYA cries out in fright.

LOPAHIN (*angrily*): How dare you? What next? Get along with you!

LYUBOV ANDREYEVNA (*hurriedly*): Take this. . . . There you are. . . . (*Searches in her purse.*) I've got no silver . . . it doesn't matter, here's a gold piece for you. . . .

PASSER-BY: God bless you, madam, very much obliged, I'm sure. (*Goes off.*)

General laughter.

VARYA (*alarmed*): I'm going . . . I'm going. . . Oh, Mamma, there is nothing to eat for the people at home and you go and give all that money to an old tramp.

LYUBOV ANDREYEVNA: What a fool I am! I'm incorri-

gible! I'll give you all I've got when we get home, everything. Yermolay Alexeyevich, you will lend me some
more, won't you?

LOPAHIN: At your service.

LYUBOV ANDREYEVNA: Come along, everyone, it's time to
go. By the way, Varya, we almost arranged your marriage,
just now. Congratulations.

VARYA (*through her tears*): You're not to joke about that,
Mamma.

LOPAHIN: 'Ophelia, get thee to a nunnery. . . .'

GAEV: My hands are shaking, it's a long time since I had my
game.

LOPAHIN: 'Ophelia, Nymph, in thine orisons be all my sins
remembered!'

LYUBOV ANDREYEVNA: Let's go, it's nearly dinner time.

VARYA: That man scared me so. My heart keeps thumping.

LOPAHIN: Just one word, please. Listen, my friends, just one
word. On the 22nd August they are going to sell the cherry
orchard. Just remember that, will you . . . think of that. . . .

Everybody goes off except TROFIMOV *and* ANYA.

ANYA (*laughing*): I'm grateful to the tramp for frightening
Varya, now we are alone at last.

TROFIMOV: Varya is afraid that we shall go and fall in love
with each other, so she follows us about all day long. Her
narrow mind won't allow her to understand that we are
above love. All that we look for and long for in life is to get
rid of the shallowness, the deceit, and all those stupid
qualities that prevent us from being free and happy. Forward.
We must advance with unshaken determination towards

the bright star that is shining far, far before us. Forward! Don't lag behind, friends.

ANYA (*stretching out her arms*): What beautiful things you say! (*Pause*.) It is glorious here today!

TROFIMOV: Yes, it's wonderful weather.

ANYA: What have you done to me, Petya, why is it I don't love the cherry orchard as I did once? I used to love it so tenderly, it seemed that there wasn't a better place on earth than our orchard.

TROFIMOV: All Russia is our orchard. The earth is great and beautiful, and full of wonderful places. (*Pause*.) Think of it, Anya! Your grandfather, your great-grandfather and all your ancestors were landowners, they owned living souls! Cannot you see human beings staring at you in the cherry orchard from every leaf, from every branch? Can't you hear their voices . . .? Oh, it is dreadful. Your orchard frightens me. When I walk through it in the evening or at night, the bark on the trees seems to glitter in the shadows, and it seems as if the cherry trees were dreaming of all that has happened these two or three hundred years. The trees seem weighed down with the sad memories of these times gone by – well, what can I say? We are at least two hundred years behind. We've achieved nothing yet, we've not made up our minds how we stand with the past, we only philosophise and complain of boredom and drink vodka. It's all so clear to me; before we can live in the present we must first redeem the past, and have done with it, and that we can only do by suffering, by unremitting toil. You must understand this, Anya.

ANYA: The house we live in hasn't really been ours for a long time, and I shall go away and leave it, I promise you.

TROFIMOV: Leave it, yes, and, if you have the keys, throw them into the well and go right away. Be free as the wind.

ANYA (*enthusiastically*): How beautifully you said that!

TROFIMOV: You must believe me, Anya! You must! I'm not thirty yet, I'm young, I'm still a student, but – I have suffered so much already. As soon as winter comes I get half-starved, and ill, and worried. I've no money. My luck has driven me from one place to another, all sorts of places, here and there, nowhere that I really belong to – yet in spite of it all I have a strange feeling that something wonderful will happen to me – all day long I feel it coming, some strange happiness. Anya, I know it will – I can see it.

ANYA (*dreamily*): The moon is rising.

One can hear EPIHODOV *playing on his guitar the same sad song. The moon rises. Somewhere near the poplars* VARYA *is looking for* ANYA, *and she calls out,* 'Anya, where are you?'

TROFIMOV: Yes, the moon is rising. (*Pause.*) There it is, happiness, there it comes nearer and nearer, I can almost hear its footsteps. And if we never see it, if we do not know it when it comes, what does it matter? Others will.

VARYA'S VOICE: Anya, where are you?

TROFIMOV: That's Varya again! (*Angry.*) It really is too bad!

ANYA: Never mind. Let's go down to the river. It's so lovely there.

TROFIMOV: Let's go.

They go.

VARYA'S VOICE: Anya! Anya!

CURTAIN

ACT THREE

SCENE: *A drawing-room separated by an arch from the ballroom.*
A chandelier is burning. One can hear the Jewish orchestra playing
in the hall, the same as the one that was mentioned in Act Two.
It is evening.
They are dancing the 'grande ronde' in the ballroom. The voice of
SEMYONOV-PISHTCHIK *saying, 'Promenade à une paire!'*
First PISHTCHIK *and* CHARLOTTA IVANOVNA *come out*
into the drawing-room, then TROFIMOV *and* LYUBOV ANDRE-
YEVNA, *thirdly* ANYA *with the* POST-OFFICE CLERK, *and*
fourthly VARYA *with the* STATION-MASTER. VARYA *is crying*
softly while she dances, and wipes her eyes. DUNYASHA *is in*
the last pair. They cross the drawing-room, and PISHTCHIK
cries out, 'Grande ronde, balancez!' *and* 'Les Cavaliers à
genoux et remerciez vos dames!'
FIRS, *in tails, brings in a tray with seltzerwater on it.*
PISHTCHIK *and* TROFIMOV *come into the drawing-room.*

PISHTCHIK: I've got high blood pressure, you know, I've
had two strokes already and I find dancing difficult, but,
as the saying goes, if you run with the pack you must bark
with the hounds. I'm as strong as a horse. My dear old
father, who loved a joke, used to say that the ancient family
of Semyonov-Pishtchik went back to the very horse that

Caligula made a senator. . . . (*He sits down.*) But the worst of it is I've no money; a starving dog longs for nothing but meat. (*He snores but wakes up almost immediately.*) I'm like that . . . I can't think of anything but money. . . .

TROFIMOV: It's true, there is something about you, you do look a bit like a horse.

PISHTCHIK: Well, what of it . . .? A horse is a good useful creature . . . you can sell a horse.

One can hear them playing billiards in the next room. VARYA *appears under the arch in the ballroom.*

TROFIMOV (*teasing*): Madame Lopahin! Madame Lopahin!

VARYA (*angrily*): Old scruffy fellow! Perpetual student!

TROFIMOV: Yes, I am. And I'm not ashamed of it!

VARYA (*in a bitter mood*): Mamma's gone and hired the Jewish orchestra, but where's the money to pay them with? (*She goes.*)

TROFIMOV (*to* PISHTCHIK): If all the energy that you have wasted finding money to pay the interest on your debts had been used for something else, you would probably have turned the whole world upside down by this time, you know.

PISHTCHIK: Nietzsche . . . the philosopher . . . very remarkable man, very famous . . . a man of tremendous intellect, remarks somewhere in his books, that it's perfectly all right to forge bank notes.

TROFIMOV: Have you ever read Nietzsche?

PISHTCHIK: No. Well . . . Not exactly. My daughter Dashenka told me. I'm in such a tricky position now I wouldn't mind forging a few bank notes myself. Tomorrow

I have to pay three hundred roubles on a bill. Thank God I've managed to borrow a hundred and thirty already. (*Feels in his pockets.*) (*In alarm.*) Oh, the money's gone! I've lost the lot! (*Through his tears.*) I can't find it anywhere! (*Gleefully.*) No, here it is – slipped down inside the lining. Oh! I'm exhausted. I'm in a muck sweat.

LYUBOV ANDREYEVNA *and* CHARLOTTA IVANOVNA *come in.*

LYUBOV ANDREYEVNA (*humming the Lezginka*): Why is Leonid so long? What is he doing in town? (*To* DUNYASHA.) Dunyasha, give the musicians some tea.

TROFIMOV: Perhaps the auction didn't take place after all.

LYUBOV ANDREYEVNA: It was the wrong day to ask the musicians to come up, the wrong day to choose to give a party . . . well, it can't be helped now. (*She sits down and hums softly.*)

CHARLOTTA IVANOVNA (*handing* PISHTCHIK *a pack of cards*): Here's a pack of cards. Here, take them. Now, think of any card you like.

PISHTCHIK: I've thought of one.

CHARLOTTA IVANOVNA: Shuffle the cards. Are they shuffled? Very well. Now, give them to me, mon cher Monsieur Pishtchik. Ein, zwei, drei! Now look for your card. You'll find it in your pocket. There now!

PISHTCHIK (*taking card out of his pocket*): The eight of spades, perfectly right. (*Amazed.*) Would you believe it? Quite extraordinary.

CHARLOTTA IVANOVNA (*holding the pack of cards at arm's length to* TROFIMOV): Tell me quickly, what is the top card?

TROFIMOV: I don't know. What?

CHARLOTTA: The top card?

TROFIMOV: Oh, all right then – the queen of spades.

CHARLOTTA IVANOVNA: Here it is. (*To* PISHTCHIK.) Now then, your turn. What card's on top?

PISHTCHIK: The ace of hearts.

CHARLOTTA IVANOVNA: Voilà! Now then, ladies and gentlemen. Watch my pack of cards very carefully, please. Un, deux, trois! Presto! (*She taps the pack of cards and they disappear.*) Shh! What lovely weather today. (*A Woman's voice answers her as though coming from the floor.*) Oh, yes, the weather is magnificent, madame. (*In her own voice.*) You are perfectly charming, delightful. (*The Voice replies*) I think you ferry peautiful too, madame.

STATION-MASTER (*applauding*): Bravo, Madame Ventriloquist, bravo!

PISHTCHIK (*astonished*): Would you believe it! My charming Charlotta Ivanovna, you're fascinating . . . really, I'm quite in love with you. . . .

CHARLOTTA IVANOVNA: In love? (*Shrugging her shoulders.*) Are you really capable of love? Guter Mensch, aber schlechter Musikant.

TROFIMOV (*slapping* PISHTCHIK *on the back*): You old horse!

CHARLOTTA IVANOVNA: Your attention for a moment, please, just one more trick. (*Taking a shawl from the chair.*) Here is a very good shawl and I'm going to sell this very pretty shawl. (*Shakes it.*) Now then! Any offers? Who'll buy? Who'll buy?

PISHTCHIK (*astonished*): Remarkable! Astonishing!

CHARLOTTA IVANOVNA: Ein, zwei, drei! Hopla!

She lifts up the stretched out shawl quickly to show ANYA *standing behind it; who curtseys, runs to her mother, kisses her and then goes back into the ballroom amid general admiration.*

LYUBOV ANDREYEVNA (*clapping*): Bravo, Charlotta, bravo!

CHARLOTTA IVANOVNA: Now let's try once more! Ein, zwei, drei! Hopla!

Lifts the rug and VARYA *is standing behind it bowing.*

PISHTCHIK (*astonished*): Would you believe it? It's astounding!

CHARLOTTA IVANOVNA: That's all. Finished! (*Throws the shawl over* PISHTCHIK, *curtseys and runs away into the other room.*)

PISHTCHIK (*running after her*): You little rascal . . . well? Well, really! Did you ever! (*He goes.*)

LYUBOV ANDREYEVNA: Still no sign of Leonid! I can't understand what he's doing all this time in town! Everything must be over by now. The estate must have been sold – or perhaps the auction hasn't taken place, but why must he keep us so long in suspense?

VARYA (*trying to calm her*): Uncle has bought it, dear Uncle Leonid, I'm sure he has.

TROFIMOV (*ironically*): Oh yes! Of course!

VARYA: Anya's great-aunt was going to send the money to buy the estate with. She's doing it for Anya's sake. I'm sure God will help us and Uncle Leonid will buy it.

LYUBOV ANDREYEVNA: Anya's aunt has sent us the money to buy the estate in *her* name – she does not trust us – but it wouldn't be enough to even pay the interest. (*Covering her face with her hands.*) My future is being decided today – my whole future.

TROFIMOV (*teasing* VARYA): Madame Lopahin.

VARYA (*angrily*): Perpetual student! You've already been sent down twice from the university.

LYUBOV ANDREYEVNA: Why do you get so cross, Varya? He's only teasing you about Lopahin. What does it matter? You can marry Lopahin if you like, he's a nice interesting man. But if you don't want to marry him, then don't, nobody's trying to force you, darling.

VARYA: Mamma, I'm very serious about all this, and I must be honest. He's a good man and I like him.

LYUBOV ANDREYEVNA: Well, marry him then, what are you waiting for? I don't understand!

VARYA: But I can't propose to him myself. For two whole years now everyone has been talking to me about him, but either he says nothing or just jokes. I understand. He's making money, he's always busy, he has no time to think of me. If only I had some money, just a very little, just a hundred roubles, I would leave everything and go away. I would go into a convent.

TROFIMOV: Such happiness!

VARYA (to TROFIMOV): A student ought to have some brains! (*In a soft voice through her tears.*) How ugly you've grown, Petya, how old and tired you look. (*To* LYUBOV ANDREYEVNA, *crying no more.*) I can't bear having no work, Mamma. I must have something to do every minute of the day.

YASHA *comes in.*

YASHA (*hardly able to restrain his laughter*): Epihodov has broken a billiard cue! (*He goes out.*)

VARYA: What is Epihodov doing here? Who gave him leave to play billiards? I don't understand these people. . . . (*Goes out.*)

LYUBOV ANDREYEVNA: Don't tease her, Petya, you can see she is upset enough as it is.

TROFIMOV: She's so officious, poking her nose into other people's business. All this summer she's given Anya and me no peace. She's terrified we might be having a love-affair. What business is it of hers, I'd like to know? It's not as if we'd ever given her the slightest excuse for her suspicions. We've no time for such trivialities. We are above love.

LYUBOV ANDREYEVNA: Well then, I must be beneath love, I suppose. Why doesn't Leonid come? If only I knew whether the estate was sold or not. It all seems so dreadful, so impossible. I'm really distracted, I don't know what to think. I could scream, do something stupid. Talk to me, Petya. Say something – anything.

TROFIMOV: It doesn't really matter, does it, whether the estate is sold today or not? It was all over long ago, it is finished, there's no turning back, the path is overgrown. Calm yourself, dear Lyubov Andreyevna. It's no use trying to deceive yourself. You might just as well face the truth.

LYUBOV ANDREYEVNA: You are so sure of what is true and what is false, but I seem to be blind, incapable of seeing anything. You seem to know the solutions to all your important problems but do remember, my dear boy, you're still young, you haven't suffered – you don't know what dreadful things life may hold in store for you. You are braver perhaps than we are, more honest and serious-minded – but you must try to be more generous in your judgements. Try to understand my feelings. This house has always been my home, I was born here – I love it so – and the cherry orchard – I can't imagine life without it. If it has to be sold let them sell me with it. My son, my Grisha (*embraces* TROFIMOV) was drowned here. (*Weeps.*) You're so good and kind-hearted, Petya. Try to understand.

TROFIMOV: You know I sympathise with all my heart.

LYUBOV ANDREYEVNA: Yes, yes, I know, but you ought to say it somehow differently. . . . (*She takes out her handkerchief and a telegram falls on to the floor.*) You can't think how dreadfully depressed I feel this evening – so much noise everywhere, it gets on my nerves, I keep imagining things. And yet I can't bear to be alone in my room, the silence frightens me. Don't be hard on me, Petya, I love you as if you were my son. I would gladly let Anya marry you, of course I would, but you must go on studying, my dear boy, you must complete your education. You don't do anything with your life. Fate seems to drive you about from one place to another. And that's not right. It's true what I say, isn't it? And you really must do something to make your beard grow properly. I can't help laughing at you.

TROFIMOV (*picking up the telegram*): I don't care what I look like.

LYUBOV ANDREYEVNA: This telegram is from Paris. I get them every day. That wretch is ill again, things are going badly for him – he asks me to forgive him, begs me to go back, and really I feel I ought to go to be near him. You look so sternly at me, Petya, but what can I do, my dear boy, what can I do? He's alone there, ill and unhappy with no one to look after him, no one to prevent him doing stupid things, and make him take his medicine at the proper times. After all, why should I be ashamed to admit it, I love him, of course I love him, I do, I do – my love for him is like a stone round my neck, dragging me down. But I love him and I can't live without him. Don't speak to me, Petya – don't say anything.

TROFIMOV: Forgive me, please, I can't bear to hurt your feelings but the man's quite unworthy of you.

LYUBOV ANDREYEVNA: No, no, no. You mustn't talk like that. (*Covers her ears.*)

TROFIMOV: But it's so obvious. Can't you see? He's spending your money, he's a fortune-hunter, an adventurer.

LYUBOV ANDREYEVNA (*angrily, but restraining herself*): You're twenty-six or twenty-seven, and you're still a student in the second class.

TROFIMOV: That has nothing to do with it.

LYUBOV ANDREYEVNA: You ought to be a man by now. At your age, you ought to be able to understand people who are in love. You ought to be in love yourself. . . . You ought to have fallen in love. (*Angrily.*) Yes, of course, you ought. It's not purity with you – you're just a prig, a ridiculous crank, a kind of freak. . . .

TROFIMOV (*in horror*): You don't know what you're saying.

LYUBOV ANDREYEVNA: 'I'm above love!' Indeed! You're not above love at all. You're simply what old Firs calls 'a muddler'. At your age you ought to have a mistress!

TROFIMOV (*in horror*): This is appalling! I won't listen. (*He quickly crosses the stage into the ballroom, clutching his head.*) I can't bear it, I'm going. (*Goes off, but returns immediately.*) Everything is over between us. (*Goes off into the ballroom.*)

LYUBOV ANDREYEVNA (*shouts after him*): Petya, wait! I was only joking! Petya!

One can hear from the hall the sound of someone quickly descending the staircase and suddenly falling with a crash. ANYA *and* VARYA *scream, but immediately after one hears laughter.*

What's the matter?

ANYA *runs in.*

ANYA (*laughing*): Petya's fallen down the back stairs. (*She runs out.*)

LYUBOV ANDREYEVNA: What a ridiculous fellow he is. . . .

The STATION-MASTER *stops in the middle of the drawing-room and reads 'The Sinners' of Tolstoy. They listen to him.*

STATION-MASTER: The lofty hall is decked and gay –
            The cymbals clash – the dancers sway;
            The sinful woman sits apart
            With guilty soul and stricken heart. . . .

A waltz interrupts him and he has to stop. Everyone dances. From the hall pass TROFIMOV, ANYA, VARYA *and* LYUBOV ANDREYEVNA.

LYUBOV ANDREYEVNA: Now, Petya, there, my dear boy, I didn't mean it, really. Please forgive me. Come and dance. . . . (*Dances with* PETYA.)

ANYA *and* VARYA *dance.* FIRS *comes in, puts his stick near the side door.* YASHA *has come in from the ballroom and watches the dance.*

YASHA: Well, Grandpa? How goes it?

FIRS: I'm not too well. In the old days at our parties we used to have generals in to dance here, barons and admirals, but now we have to send for the post-office clerk and the station-master, and even they only come as a favour. I seem to be getting so much weaker lately. My old master, the mistress's grandfather, I mean, used to give everyone powdered sealing wax for medicine, no matter what the illness was. I've been taking it every day for the last twenty years or more; maybe that's why I am alive.

YASHA: I'm sick of you, grandpa. (*Yawning.*) I wish you'd hurry up and die.

FIRS: Eh, you young muddler. (*Muttering.*)

TROFIMOV *and* LYUBOV ANDREYEVNA *dance first in the ballroom and then in the drawing-room.*

LYUBOV ANDREYEVNA: Merci, I'll sit down for a little. . . . (*Sitting.*) I'm tired.

ANYA *comes in.*

ANYA (*excited*): There was somebody in the kitchen just now saying that the cherry orchard was sold today.

LYUBOV ANDREYEVNA: Sold. To whom?

ANYA: He didn't say. He's gone now. (*She dances with* TROFIMOV *into the ballroom.*)

YASHA: It was some old man gossiping. A stranger.

FIRS: Leonid Andreyevich still not here, he's not back yet. He's only wearing that light coat, demi-saison, he'll catch cold. Tch. Ah, these youngsters!

LYUBOV ANDREYEVNA: This is unbearable. Yasha, go and find out what has happened. Ask them who bought it.

YASHA: It's too late now, the old man's been gone hours ago. (*Laughs.*)

LYUBOV ANDREYEVNA (*slightly annoyed*): What are you laughing at? What are you so pleased about?

YASHA: Epihodov is such a funny one. He's so stupid. Twenty-two misfortunes.

LYUBOV ANDREYEVNA: Firs, where will you go if the estate is sold?

FIRS: I'll go wherever you tell me.

LYUBOV ANDREYEVNA: Why are you looking so white? Are you ill? You ought to be in bed. . . .

FIRS: Oh yes! Bed. And who's to serve the guests if I go to bed? Who'll look after everything? There's no one to look after the house but me.

YASHA (*to* LYUBOV ANDREYEVNA): Lyubov Andreyevna! Permit me to ask you a favour; if you go back again to Paris will you please be so kind as to take me with you? (*Looking round and in a lower tone.*) It's quite impossible to stay here. What's the use of talking? You can see for yourself. This is a barbarous country, the people really have no morals at all; and besides it's so dull. They feed us abominably downstairs. And there's old Firs to put up with, shuffling about, making stupid remarks. . . . Take me away with you, please, will you?

PISHTCHIK *comes in.*

PISHTCHIK: Allow me to ask you for a little waltz, beautiful lady.

LYUBOV ANDREYEVNA *accepts.*

All the same, my enchantress, I will have that hundred and eighty roubles from you if you please ... I will borrow ... (*Dancing.*) the small sum of a hundred and eighty roubles to pay the interest on my mortgage.

They pass into the ballroom.

YASHA (*humming softly*): 'O wilt thou understand the torments of my soul?'

In the ballroom one can see a person in a grey top hat and check trousers, gesticulating and jumping about; one hears cries of 'Bravo, Charlotta Ivanovna.'

DUNYASHA (*stopping to powder her nose*): My young lady tells me I'm to dance – there are so many gentlemen and so few ladies, but dancing makes my head go round and my heart beats so fast, Firs Nikoleyevich. The gentleman from the post-office told me something just now that quite took my breath away.

The music dies down.

FIRS: What was that?

DUNYASHA: 'You're like a flower.' That's what he said.

YASHA (*yawning*): Common fellow! (*Goes out.*)

DUNYASHA: 'Like a flower' ... I'm so sensitive, I love it when people say nice things to me.

FIRS: You'll come to a bad end, my girl.

EPIHODOV *comes in.*

EPIHODOV: You seem to wish to avoid me, Avdotya Fedorovna, as if I were some sort of insect. ... (*Sighs.*) That's life.

DUNYASHA: Well, what is it?

EPIHODOV: You may be right, of course, But on the other

hand, if you look at it from a certain point of view, I must inform you that you've driven me into such a state. I quite appreciate my destiny, every day some new misfortune happens to me, but I got used to that state of affairs long ago, and face my fortune with a smile. You've given me your word and even if I. . . .

DUNYASHA: Please, please, let's talk about that another time. Leave me alone now, I'm dreaming. (*Playing with her fan.*)

EPIHODOV: Some misfortune or other happens to me every day, and yet, if I may so express myself, I simply smile, I even laugh.

> VARYA *comes in from the ballroom.*

VARYA: Haven't you gone yet, Semyon? Really what a disrespectful fellow you are. (*To* DUNYASHA.) Be off with you, Dunyasha. (*To* EPIHODOV.) First you play billiards and break a cue, and now here you are strolling about the drawing-room like a visitor.

EPIHODOV: Allow me to tell you you can't start taking it out of me like that.

VARYA: I'm not taking it out of you, I'm simply telling you. You know very well you just go wandering about from place to place doing absolutely nothing. What on earth we keep a clerk for Heaven only knows.

EPIHODOV (*offended*): Whether I work or whether I walk, whether I eat or whether I play billiards, the only people who can sit in judgement on me are those who understand me, or those who are my superiors.

VARYA: How dare you talk to me like that! (*Getting angrier.*) How dare you! I don't understand things, don't I? Get out of here! At once! Do you hear?

EPIHODOV (*frightened*): I do wish you would make use of more refined expressions.

VARYA (*quite beside herself*): Get out of here! Get out this very minute!

He goes towards the door and she follows him.

Twenty-two misfortunes! Make yourself scarce! Get out of my sight!

EPIHODOV: I'll make a complaint about you. (*He has gone out and one hears his voice behind the door.*)

VARYA: Ah! You're coming back, are you! (*Takes the stick* FIRS *has put near the side door.*) Come on . . . come on . . . come on. I'll show you. . . . Ah! You're coming back? I dare you to! All right then, take that!

VARYA *brandishes the stick and at that moment* LOPAHIN *comes in, she hits him on the head.*

LOPAHIN: Many thanks. Much obliged.

VARYA (*angry and laughing*): I'm sorry.

LOPAHIN: Don't mention it. Thank you for such a charming welcome.

VARYA: No need to thank me. (*She moves away and then looking round she asks gently*) I didn't hurt you, did I?

LOPAHIN: No, it's nothing. I shall have a huge bump to-morrow, that's all.

VOICES (*in the ballroom*): Lopahin has arrived! Yermolay Alexeyevich!

PISHTCHIK: What a sight for sore eyes. . . . (*Kisses* LOPAHIN.) You smell of cognac, my dear soul. We're enjoying ourselves here, too. Having a high old time.

LYUBOV ANDREYEVNA *comes in.*

LYUBOV ANDREYEVNA: Yermolay Alexeyevich, at last you've come. Why have you been so long? Where's Leonid?

LOPAHIN: Leonid Andreyevich came back with me. He'll be here in a moment. . . .

LYUBOV ANDREYEVNA (*excitedly*): Well, what happened? Did the sale take place? Tell me. . . .

LOPAHIN (*embarrassed; afraid to show his pleasure*): The sale finished about four o'clock . . . we missed the train though, had to wait till half past nine. (*Sighs heavily.*) Ough! My head's going round. . . .

GAEV *comes in, holding some parcels in his right hand and wiping his eyes with his left.*

LYUBOV ANDREYEVNA: Leonid, what happened? Well, Leonid? (*Impatiently, with tears.*) Quickly, for God's sake, tell me.

GAEV (*not answering her, only waving his hand and in a plaintive tone to* FIRS): There, take these . . . there are some anchovies, Kertch herrings. . . . I've had nothing to eat all day. . . . Lord, what I've been through. . . .

The door of the billiard room opens. One can hear the click of billiard balls.
I'm so frightfully tired.

YASHA (*from the billiard room*): Thirteen and five – eighteen.

GAEV (*his expression changes completely. He is no longer crying*): Come and help me to change, Firs. (*He crosses the back of the stage to go to his room followed by* FIRS.)

PISHTCHIK: Well, what about the sale? Come on, tell us about it.

LYUBOV ANDREYEVNA: Was the cherry orchard sold?

LOPAHIN: Yes.

LYUBOV ANDREYEVNA: Who bought it?

LOPAHIN: I did.

A pause. LYUBOV ANDREYEVNA *is devastated; she falls down if she weren't leaning against an armchair.*

VARYA *takes the keys from her belt and throws them into the middle of the room, and departs.*

LOPAHIN: I bought it. Now, now, ladies and gentlemen, wait a moment please. Don't rush me. My head's all in a muddle. I can't speak yet. (*Laughs.*) When we got to the auction Deriganov was there already. Of course Leonid Andreyevich only had fifteen thousand and Deriganov started by bidding thirty thousand at once, in addition to the arrears. I could see how things were going, so I bid against him and offered forty thousand. He bid forty-five, I bid fifty-five. He kept adding five thousand each time and I would add ten. Up and up it went. Well, at last it was all over. I bid nine thousand over and above the mortgage and got the property. (*Chuckles.*) The cherry orchard is mine now! Mine! My God, ladies and gentlemen, the cherry orchard is mine! Tell me that I am drunk, out of my mind, this is all imagination. . . . (*Stamps his feet.*) Don't laugh at me! Imagine if my father and grandfather rose from their graves and saw all that has happened, how their little Yermolay, the lad they used to whip, who could hardly read or write, and ran about barefoot all the winter, how he's risen to buy this estate, the most beautiful place on God's earth! I've bought the estate where my father and grand-father were serfs, where they were not even allowed into the kitchen. I must be asleep, it's all a dream, I can't believe it. It's all a trick of my imagination, wrapped in the mists of ignorance. (*Picks up the keys and smiles gently.*) She threw the keys down to show she isn't the housekeeper any longer. (*He clinks the key.*) Well, what does it matter?

One hears the orchestra tuning the instruments.

Eh? Musicians! Strike up. Play something! I want to hear you. Now then, all of you, come and see Yermolay Lopahin take his axe to the cherry orchard, how the trees will come crashing down! We will build villas and our grandsons and great-grandsons will see a new living world growing up here. . . . Come on, louder, let's have more music!

Orchestra plays. LYUBOV ANDREYEVNA *has collapsed into the chair and is weeping bitterly.*

LOPAHIN (*reproachfully*): Why, but why didn't you listen to me in time? My poor dear, you can't alter it now. (*With tears in his eyes.*) If only all this was over, if only this unhappy topsy-turvy life of ours would change.

PISHTCHIK (*taking him by the arm and in an undertone*): She's crying. . . . Let's go into the other room and leave her alone . . . come along. (*Takes him by the arm and leads him away.*)

LOPAHIN: What's the matter? Music! Play louder! Everything must as I want it now! (*Ironically.*) Here comes the new master, the owner of the cherry orchard. (*He knocks a little table over accidentally, and nearly upsets a candelabrum.*) Never mind. I can pay for everything. (*Goes out with* PISHTCHIK.)

No one is left either in the ballroom or the drawing-room except LYUBOV ANDREYEVNA, *who remains sitting, crumpled up*

and weeping. The music plays softly. ANYA *and* TROFIMOV
enter quickly. ANYA *goes to her mother and kneels beside her.*
TROFIMOV *remains at the entrance of the drawing-room.*

ANYA: Mamma . . .! Mamma, you're crying? My dear, kind,
sweet, good Mamma, my beautiful Mamma, I love you. . . .
I bless you. The cherry orchard is sold, it doesn't exist any
more. That's true, only don't cry, Mamma. You still have
your life before you, your dear innocent heart. . . . Come
away with me, come my darling, come away from here. . .!
We will plant a new orchard, more beautiful than this one.
You will see, you will understand, your heart will be filled
with happiness, like the sun in the evening. And then you
will smile again, Mamma. Come with me, my darling,
come with me. . . .

CURTAIN

ACT FOUR

SCENE: *Same as Act One.*

There are no curtains at the windows, no pictures, only a few pieces of furniture, which are stacked in one corner as if for sale. There is an impression of emptiness. Near the front door and at the back of the stage stand trunks, travelling bags and so on. On the left the door is open and one can hear the voices of VARYA *and* ANYA.

LOPAHIN *stands and waits.* YASHA *is holding a tray of glasses filled with champagne. In the hall* EPIHODOV *is cording a crate. Behind the wall (back) there is the sound of voices. These are the peasants who have come to say good-bye. The voice of* GAEV, 'Thank you, my friends, thank you!'*

YASHA: The peasants have come to say good-bye. I am of opinion, Yermolay Alexeyevich, that they are kind-hearted people, but they understand very little.

The buzz of talk dies down. LYUBOV ANDREYEVNA *and* GAEV *come through the hall; she is not crying, but is very pale, her face is convulsed and she cannot speak.*

GAEV: You gave them your purse, Lyuba. You shouldn't have done that! You really shouldn't.

LYUBOV ANDREYEVNA: I couldn't help it! I couldn't help it!
Both go out.

LOPAHIN (*at the door, calls after them*): Come back a minute, won't you? Have some champagne? Please. Just one glass to say good-bye. I didn't think of bringing some from town, and they only had one bottle at the station. Do, please! (*Pause.*) Come along! Don't you want some? (*Moves away from the door.*) If I had known – I wouldn't have bought any. Very well then, I don't want it either.

  YASHA *puts the tray carefully on a chair.*
You have a drink, Yasha, if nobody else will.

YASHA: *Bon voyage.* And here's to the ones who stay behind! (*Drinks.*) This champagne isn't the real thing, I can tell you.

LOPAHIN: Eight roubles a bottle. (*Pause.*) It's devilish cold here.

YASHA: We didn't light the stoves today; it doesn't matter as we're leaving. (*Laughs.*)

LOPAHIN: What are you laughing for?

YASHA: Just pleasure.

LOPAHIN: Here we are in October, but it's quiet and sunny as if it were summer. Good building weather. (*Looking at clock, then speaking through the door.*) Ladies and gentlemen, remember you've only forty-seven minutes before the train goes! It means you must leave here in twenty minutes! Don't be long now.

  TROFIMOV *comes in from outside in his coat.*

TROFIMOV: I think it's nearly time to start. The carriages are round. I can't think where the deuce my goloshes are. They've simply disappeared. . . . (*Through the door.*) Anya! My goloshes aren't here! I can't find them.

LOPAHIN: I have to go to Harkov. I'll start in the same train as you. I'm going to spend the winter in Harkov. I've wasted a lot of time with you people; I'm quite lost without work to occupy me. I can't exist without a job; I don't know what to do with my hands, they dangle about as though they didn't belong to me.

TROFIMOV: We'll soon be gone now, and then you will be able to start again on your useful labours.

LOPAHIN: Have a drink, just a small glass, do.

TROFIMOV: I won't, thank you.

LOPAHIN: You're off to Moscow, aren't you?

TROFIMOV: Yes, I'll see them as far as town, and then to-morrow I'll go on to Moscow, to the University.

LOPAHIN: Well, well. . . . I suppose the professors haven't started their lectures yet . . . they're waiting for you to arrive.

TROFIMOV: It's none of your business.

LOPAHIN: How many years is it now that you have been a student?

TROFIMOV: Think of a new one, can't you? That joke is as old as Methuselah. (*Looking for his goloshes.*) By the way, in case we don't see each other again, allow me to give you one piece of advice before I go. Don't flap your hands about. Get out of your habit of flapping. And another thing, this talk of building villas, this certainty you have about summer residents turning into small freeholders, all that sort of thing is flapping too. . . . But all the same I like you. You have got fine sensitive fingers like an artist; yes, you're a fine, sensitive soul. . . .

LOPAHIN (*embracing him*): Good-bye, my dear fellow. Thank you for everything. If you need money for the journey I can let you have some.

TROFIMOV: What should I need money for?

LOPAHIN: But you haven't got any.

TROFIMOV: Yes, I have, thank you. I've just been paid for a translation. It's here in my pocket. (*Anxiously.*) But I can't find my goloshes anywhere.

VARYA (*from the other room*): Here! take your rubbish! (*Throws a pair of goloshes into the room.*)

TROFIMOV: Why do you get so angry, Varya . . . ? But these aren't my goloshes!

LOPAHIN: I sowed five hundred acres of poppies this Spring, and it has brought me a clear profit of forty thousand roubles. And when my poppies were all in flower, what a picture they made! As I say, I cleared forty thousand, that means I am offering you money because I've got it to spare. Why are you so stuck up? I'm just a peasant . . . it's from the heart.

TROFIMOV: Your father was a peasant, mine owned a chemist's shop. That doesn't prove anything.

LOPAHIN *takes out his pocket book.*

No, no, I tell you I don't want it! Even if you offered me twenty thousand I wouldn't take it. I'm an independent person. What you admire and value, all of you, rich or poor, doesn't carry the slightest weight with me, it's like thistledown blowing in the wind. I can do without you; I can pass you by; I'm proud and strong. Humanity is advancing towards the highest truth, towards the greatest happiness that can exist on earth, and I'm in the foremost ranks.

LOPAHIN: Will you ever get there?

TROFIMOV: Yes. (*Pause.*) I shall get there or I shall show others the way.

In the distance one hears the stroke of an axe on the trees.
Well, good-bye, my dear fellow. It's time to go. We turn up our noses at one another, but meanwhile life is slipping by. When I work hard with no time to rest, then my thoughts are clearer, and I too seem to understand why I am alive. How many people in Russia, my friend, exist to no purpose whatever. Well, never mind. Leonid Andreyevich has accepted a place in the bank, at six thousand roubles a year . . . he'll never stick it, he's so lazy. . . .
ANYA *appears in the doorway.*

ANYA: Mamma says will you please not cut down the cherry orchard while she's still here.

TROFIMOV: Really, haven't you got that much tact! (*Goes out into the hall.*)

LOPAHIN: Yes, yes, of course, I'll see to it at once . . . what fools they are really. . . . (*Follows him.*)

ANYA: Has Firs been sent to hospital?

YASHA: I told them this morning. He's gone by now, I expect.

ANYA (*to* EPIHODOV, *who is crossing the room*): Semyon Pantaleyevich, please find out if they've taken Firs to hospital.

YASHA (*offended*): I said I told Yegor this morning, what's the use of asking ten times over?

EPIHODOV: It is my final considered opinion that old Firs is beyond repair; he ought to be gathered to his forefathers. I can only envy him. (*Puts a trunk down on a cardboard hat-box and squashes it*.) Well, there you are, you see, I might have known it. (*Goes out*.)

YASHA: (*laughing*) Twenty-two misfortunes.

VARYA(*from behind the door*): Have they taken Firs to hospital?

ANYA: Yes.

VARYA: Why haven't they taken the letter for the doctor, then?

ANYA: I'll send someone after them with it. (*Goes out*.)

VARYA (*from the next room*): Tell Yasha that his mother is here, she wants to say good-bye to him.

YASHA (*with a gesture of his hand*): Oh! She's enough to try the patience of a saint.

　　All this time DUNYASHA *has been standing by the trunk; now that* YASHA *is left alone she comes up to him.*

DUNYASHA: You might just look at me, once, Yasha. Fancy going away . . . leaving me behind. . . . (*Cries and throws herself on his neck*.)

YASHA: What's the use of crying? (*Drinks some champagne*.) In six days' time I'll be back in Paris. Tomorrow we'll get into the express and off we'll go, just as if we'd never been here at all. I can hardly believe it. 'Veeve la France!' I can't stay here, it doesn't suit me . . . that is all there is to it. I've had enough of the simple life. I'm fed up with it. What are you crying for? Just behave yourself like a respectable girl, and then there won't be any need to cry.

DUNYASHA (*looking into the mirror and powdering herself*): Write me a letter from Paris. You see I loved you, Yasha, I did love you so much. I'm such a soft-hearted creature. Yasha.

YASHA: Somebody's coming!

YASHA busies himself with the trunks, humming softly.
LYUBOV ANDREYEVNA, GAEV, ANYA and CHARLOTTA
IVANOVNA come in.

GAEV: We ought to be off soon. There's very little time left.
(*Looking at* YASHA.) Somebody smells of fish.

LYUBOV ANDREYEVNA: In about ten minutes' time we shall
have to take our places in the carriages. (*Casts a look round
the room.*) Good-bye, dear old house. Winter will pass,
spring will come, and you won't be here any more; they
are going to pull you down. Oh, think of all these walls
have seen! (*Kisses her daughter passionately.*) My little treasure,
how radiant you are, your eyes are shining like two stars.
Are you glad? Very glad?

ANYA: Yes, very. A new life is beginning, Mamma.

GAEV (*gaily*): She's quite right, you know, everything's much
better now. Before the cherry orchard was sold we were
all so worried and upset, but now that it's all settled and
there's no going back on it, we've calmed down and we're
almost cheerful. I've got a job in the bank. I'm a financier . . .
pot the white . . . and as for you, Lyuba, you're looking ever
so much better these days you really are, you can't deny it.

LYUBOV ANDREYEVNA: Yes, it's true my nerves are better.
(*Her coat and hat are handed to her.*) I sleep well now. Take my
things out, Yasha. It's time to go. (*To* ANYA.) My dear little
girl, we will see each other again very soon. . . . I'm going
to Paris and I shall live there on the money your great-aunt
sent to buy the estate with, yes, God bless your great-aunt –
but I'm afraid the money won't last very long.

ANYA: You'll come back soon, Mamma, won't you? I'll work so hard at school to pass my examinations and afterwards I shall be able to work properly and help you. We will read all sorts of books together . . . won't we, Mamma? (*Kissing her mother's hands.*) We'll read in the autumn evenings – heaps of books, and a wonderful new world will open before us. . . . (*Pensively.*) Mamma, promise you'll come back. . . .

LYUBOV ANDREYEVNA: I will, my treasure, I promise. (*Embraces her.*)

LOPAHIN *comes in.* CHARLOTTA IVANOVNA *softly sings a little song.*

GAEV: Charlotta is happy! She is singing!

CHARLOTTA IVANOVNA: (*taking a bundle that looks like a wrapped up baby*): Sleep, my little one, sleep.

(*One hears the cry of the child:* 'Yaya, Yaya!')
Be quiet, my pretty, be a good little boy!
('Yaya, Yaya!')
I'm so sorry for you, Baba. (*Throws the bundle on the luggage.*) You must find me another situation, please. I can't do without one.

LOPAHIN: We'll find you something, Charlotta Ivanovna, don't worry yourself.

GAEV: Everybody's leaving, Varya's going away . . . Suddenly nobody seems to want us.

CHARLOTTA IVANOVNA: I've nowhere to live in town. One has to go somewhere. (*Hums.*) What's the odds?

PISHTCHIK *comes in.*

PISHTCHIK: My friends!

LOPAHIN: Nature's masterpiece!

PISHTCHIK (*panting*): Oh, let me get my breath. . . . I'm quite exhausted . . . my honoured friends . . . give me some water.

GAEV: After money again, I suppose? I have a little matter to attend to. Excuse me, please. (*He goes.*)

PISHTCHIK: It's a long time since I came to see you, honoured lady. (*To* LOPAHIN.) So you're here. . . . I'm glad to see you, you're a man of great intelligence. Here, take this, accept it. (*Gives* LOPAHIN *money.*) Four hundred roubles. . . . I still owe you eight hundred and forty. . . .

LOPAHIN (*shrugs his shoulders incredulously*): I simply can't believe my eyes. Where did you get it?

PISHTCHIK: Wait a moment . . . it's so hot . . . an extraordinary coincidence. Some Englishmen came to see my property and found some sort of white clay in the ground. (*To* LYUBOV ANDREYEVNA.) And for you, beautiful, gracious lady, four hundred. . . . (*Gives her money.*) The rest will come later. (*Drinks water.*) Just now in the train a young man was telling me that some sort of great philosopher advises jumping off the roof. 'Jump!' says he, 'and that settles all problems.' (*Astonished.*) Just think of that! Water!

LOPAHIN: Who are these Englishmen you spoke of?

PISHTCHIK: I've leased them the plot of land with the clay for twenty-four years. . . . And now, excuse me, I've no more time, I must dash off. I have to go to Znoikovs, and then to the Kardamanovs, I owe everybody money. (*Drinks.*) I wish you all good day! I'll look in again on Thursday. . . .

LYUBOV ANDREYEVNA: We are just moving into town, Semyon Pishtchik, and tomorrow I go abroad.

PISHTCHIK: What! (*Agitated.*) Going to town? Why, what's happened to the furniture ... trunks ... well, never mind. ... (*Through his tears.*) It can't be helped. ... They're very intelligent people, these English – never mind . . . be happy ... God will help you ... never mind ... everything comes to an end on this earth. (*Kissing* LYUBOV ANDRE-YEVNA'S *hand.*) And if ever news should reach you that I have come to an end, give a thought to the old horse, and say, 'Once upon a time there lived a certain Semyonov-Pishtchik, the kingdom of Heaven be his . . .' Remarkable weather we're having ... yes. (*Goes out, moved, but comes back immediately and says from the doorway*) My daughter, Dashenka, sends her best regards to you. (*Goes out.*)

LYUBOV ANDREYEVNA: Well, we can go now, but I still have one or two things on my mind. The first is poor old Firs being taken ill. (*She looks at her watch*) We've still another five minutes left.

ANYA: Firs has already been taken to the hospital, Mamma. Yasha sent him off this morning.

LYUBOV ANDREYEVNA: The other is Varya. She has always been used to getting up early and working, and now she's nothing to do she's like a fish out of water. She is so thin and pale, and she keeps crying, poor dear. . . . (*A pause.*) You know very well, Yermolay Alexeyevich, I hoped to marry her to you, indeed, everything looked as if you were thinking of marrying her.

She whispers to ANYA, *who makes a sign to* CHARLOTTA IVANOVNA, *and the two go out.*

She loves you, you like her, and I can't think, I really can't conceive why you seem to avoid each other. I don't understand it.

LOPAHIN: To tell you the truth I don't understand it either. It all seems rather odd somehow. . . . If there's still time I'm quite agreeable. . . . Let's do it at once and be done with it. Without you here I feel I shall never be able to make the proposal.

LYUBOV ANDREYEVNA: Excellent. After all it will only take a minute. I will call her now.

LOPAHIN: There's some champagne here; quite suitable for the occasion.

LYUBOV ANDREYEVNA: Perfect!

LOPAHIN (*looks at the glasses*): Why! It's empty! Someone's drunk it all.

YASHA *coughs.*

LOPAHIN: That's what some people call greed . . . lapping it up like that.

LYUBOV ANDREYEVNA (*eagerly*): We will leave you alone. . . . Yasha, allez! I will call her. . . . (*Through the doors.*) Varya, leave all that and come here a moment. Come, I want you!

Goes out with YASHA.

LOPAHIN (*looking at his watch*): Yes. . . .

A pause.

Behind the doors there is suppressed laughter and whispering, and at length VARYA *comes in.*

VARYA (*looks at the things for a long time*): Funny, I can't find it anywhere.

LOPAHIN: What are you looking for?

VARYA: I packed it myself, and I can't remember which of the boxes.

Pause.

LOPAHIN: Where will you go, now Varvara Mikhailovna?

VARYA: I? To the Ragulins. I've arranged to look after things for them – as a sort of housekeeper.

LOPAHIN: That's at Yashnevo. About seventy versts from here. (*Pause.*) Well, life has come to an end in this house. . . .

VARYA (*looking at the luggage*): Where could it be . . .? Perhaps I packed it in the trunk. . . . Yes, life in this house has come to an end – there won't be any more. . . .

LOPAHIN: I have to leave for Harkov now . . . by the same train as you. I've business to do. I'm leaving Epihodov here to look after the place – I've taken him on.

VARYA: Have you?

LOPAHIN: This time last year it was snowing already if you remember; but today it's still and sunny. All the same it's cold . . . three degrees of frost.

VARYA: I didn't look. (*Pause.*) Besides the thermometer is broken.

Pause.

A voice from the yard: 'Yermolay Alexeyevich.'

LOPAHIN (*as if he's been waiting for the call for a long time*): I'm just coming!

Goes out quickly.

VARYA, *sitting on the floor, puts her head on a bundle of clothing and sobs quietly.*

The door opens. Looking around, LYUBOV ANDREYEVNA *enters carefully.*

LYUBOV: Well? (*Pause.*) We must leave.

VARYA (*stops crying and wipes her eyes*): Yes, it's time to go. I'll just be able to get to the Ragulins today, if the train isn't late. . . .

LYUBOV ANDREYEVNA (*at the door*): Anya, put your coat on.

ANYA *comes in, followed by* GAEV *and* CHARLOTTA IVA-NOVNA. GAEV *is wearing a warm coat with a Caucasian cowl. Servants come in, and the* COACHMAN. EPIHODOV *busies himself with the luggage.*

Now we can start on our journey.

ANYA: Yes, our journey. (*Happily.*)

GAEV: My good friends, my dear beloved friends! Now as I leave this house for ever, can I be silent? Can I refrain from expressing those emotions which fill my whole being at such a moment. . . .

ANYA (*imploringly*): Uncle!

VARYA: Dear uncle, what's the good?

GAEV (*dejectedly*): Double the white into the centre. I'll hold my tongue. . . .

TROFIMOV *comes in, then* LOPAHIN.

TROFIMOV: Well, ladies and gentlemen, it's time to go.

LOPAHIN: Epihodov, my coat!

LYUBOV ANDREYEVNA: I must sit here a moment longer. I feel as if I'd never noticed the walls and the ceilings of this room before, now I look at them with such tenderness, such memories. . . .

GAEV: I remember when I was six years old, on Trinity Sunday, sitting at this very window, watching father starting out for church. . . .

LYUBOV ANDREYEVNA: Has everything been taken out?

LOPAHIN: Everything, I think. (*To* EPIHODOV, *while he is putting on his coat.*) Now, Epihodov, see that everything's properly looked after.

EPIHODOV (*in a husky voice*): That'll be all right, Yermolay Alexeyevich.

LOPAHIN: What's the matter with your voice?

EPIHODOV: I was just having a drink of water and I swallowed something.

YASHA (*contemptuously*): Idiot!

LYUBOV ANDREYEVNA: We are going . . . not a soul will be left here. . . .

LOPAHIN: Until the spring.

VARYA (*pulling an umbrella out of a bundle, and looking as if she's brandishing it;* LOPAHIN *pretends to be frightened*): What? What's the matter . . . I didn't mean anything. . . .

TROFIMOV: Into the carriage, now, ladies first – we must be off. The train will be in directly.

VARYA: Petya, here are your goloshes, I found them by the portmanteau. . . . (*With tears.*) Oh! What dirty old things they are. . . .

TROFIMOV (*putting on his goloshes*): Let's go, ladies and gentlemen.

GAEV (*profoundly moved, afraid of crying*): The train . . . the station . . . yes. Cross to the centre, double the white into the pocket.

LYUBOV ANDREYEVNA: Come, everyone.

LOPAHIN: Is everybody here? No one left in there? (*Calling, then locking the little side door on the left.*) There are a lot of things stacked away in here. I'd better lock them up. Come along.

ANYA: Good-bye, house! Good-bye, old life!

TROFIMOV: Welcome new life!

> TROFIMOV *goes out with* ANYA.
>
> VARYA *looks round the room and goes out slowly.* YASHA *and* CHARLOTTA IVANOVNA *with her dog go out.*

LOPAHIN: Well, until the spring. Come, my friends . . . till we meet again! (*Goes out.*)

> LYUBOV ANDREYEVNA *and* GAEV *are left alone. It is as if they had waited for this moment. They throw themselves on each other's necks and sob quietly, afraid that they will be overheard.*

GAEV (*in despair*): Sister, dear sister.

LYUBOV ANDREYEVNA: My beloved, lovely orchard . . . My life, my youth, my happiness, good-bye. . . . Good-bye!

ANYA'S VOICE (*calling gently*): Mamma!

TROFIMOV'S VOICE (*gay – excited*): Aa – – – – –oo!

LYUBOV ANDREYEVNA: One last look at the walls, at the windows . . . our dear mother used to love walking up and down this room. . . .

GAEV: Sister, sister!

ANYA'S VOICE: Mamma!

TROFIMOV'S VOICE: Aa – – – – – oo!

LYUBOV ANDREYEVNA: We're coming!

> *They go out. The stage is empty. One hears all the doors being locked and the noise of the departing carriage. Everything becomes quiet. In the silence there is the dull sound of the stroke of an axe on a tree, monotonous and sad. One hears footsteps.*

FIRS *appears from the right. He is dressed as usual – in a cutaway coat and a waistcoat – with slippers on his feet. He looks ill.*

FIRS (*going to the door and trying the handle*): Locked! They've gone. They've forgotten about me. (*Sits on sofa.*) Never mind. I'll sit here for a bit. Leonid Andreyevich is sure to have put on his thin coat instead of his fur one. I wasn't there to look after him . . . oh, these young people. . . . (*He mumbles something one cannot understand.*) Life has passed by as though I had never lived. . . . (*Lies down.*) I'll lie down for a little. . . . You've no strength, nothing left, nothing. . . . Ech, you old muddler. (*He lies motionless.*)

One hears a far-away sound as if from the sky, like a breaking string, which dies away mournfully. Then there is silence, and one hears only the sound, far away in the cherry orchard, of an axe felling a tree.

CURTAIN